Neu Feather Dan

Stories from BLANKETS MOUNTAIN

Year one – My Forever Home

Eric and Amanda Fish

Dedicated in loving memory to:

Michelle Zoellner-Starnes
1980-2018

This book is a memoir written from the first person perspective of a cat which in and of itself makes this a work of fiction. It reflects the author's present recollections of experiences over time. Some names and characteristics have been changed, some events have been compressed and some dialogue has been recreated. Some character names have been changed.

Copyright file US Copyright Office Eric and Amanda Fish

Images and photography by Eric and Amanda Fish

KDP ISBN: 9781092204439
Imprint: Independently published

Chapter One – Furever Homes

Hai my furiends! I had a good day today. Earlier I got a notion and decided to… Oh wait, I'm sorry, I just realized that many of you already know me but there are a lot of you who I have not met yet. Well let me introduce myself.

I'm Neuro Dan – Feather Dan. I'm a tiny orange cat with a really big love for life. I know my name is a little strange but it's a big part of my story. Mum says I am her "little miracle kitty" and dad calls me his "little buddy" but most folks just call me Neuro Dan or Feather Dan. I like either and I love talking to my friends and telling them my stories. If you have a moment I would very much enjoy telling you the story of how I got that strange name. I've got lots of other stories I'd love to share too but I'll start with my name and why mum calls me her "little miracle kitty".

When I was just a kitten, I was rescued from a hoarding situation where I had been severely neglected. Mum said that was miracle number one. I was taken to an animal shelter but because of my "special needs" I was put on the list to be euthanized. I knew my days were numbered and I was very scared.

Oops, I just realized I did it again! I forgot to tell you what my "special needs" are. I'm so used to telling my stories to friends who already know this par that I forget to tell new people. Then there are times when I just get really excited that I have friends who want listen to my stories and I get ahead of myself. I will try to remember all of my *new* friends and be sure not to leave anything out.

I have neurological problems which cause me to have trouble walking…and sometimes I am told I sit funny. My muscles don't always cooperate with me and I am not very coordinated when trying to get around. The front half of my body is affected the most. My front legs don't have enough coordination for me to be able to jump down or run. I fall on my face when I try jumping down from things and that can be embarrassing if other kitties are looking. My shoulder muscles are very weak and my shoulder blades sometimes rub together when I walk, which doesn't feel very good. I don't complain much though because it doesn't really do any good to complain. I just do the best I can and love life. Mum says that my positive cattitude and determination not to let my condition get in the way of enjoying life inspire her every day. Okay, now that you know what my "special needs" are I will continue with my story.

I was rescued from the animal shelter just in time! Mum said that was miracle number two. My rescuers were wonderful people who ran a cat rescue named Easter the Extraordinarily Optimistic Kitten of Misfit Critter Farm and Sanctuary. They would save kitties that were abandoned or in animal shelters and about to be euthanized. The Misfit rescuers would care for the kitties and make sure they all got the medical attention they needed and then try to find them Furever Homes. What a wonderful thing for them to do and I was really grateful for them.

A sweet lady named KT ran Misfit Critters Farm. She took care of me as best as she could. She made sure I got all the shots I was supposed to have, made sure I got fed and even gave me treats! She was the best at giving me lots of love and petting me because she knew I was having a hard time fitting in at the rescue. With a name like Misfit Critter Farm and Sanctuary I thought for sure that I would fit in perfectly, but sometimes things don't always work out how we had first expected. Even though I thought that my "special needs" would be a natural fit in a place like Misfit, I got bullied by some of the other older cats.

KT made sure I had a safe place to hang out and that I had soft beds to sleep in. She even got me my very own pineapple to sleep in and I loved it. It was a big plush hollow pineapple with a super comfortable bed inside. When I curled up in it I was sheltered and none of the other cats could sneak up on me while I was asleep. She would take time every day and play with me too. Sometimes while she was petting me and giving me belly rubs, she would tell me that she was working super hard at finding me a Furever Home and a family of my own. Oh yeah... I absolutely love to have my belly rubbed! I purr so loud it sounds like I'm singing the song of my people.

Back then, I could actually run a little bit. And when I did, KT said I looked like a race car with square wheels. She said I looked like a drag race car with my head down near the ground and my butt up in the air and legs moving as fast as I could possibly move them. That was when I got my name; well the first half of my name anyway. When KT first rescued me, she was going to call me Lieutenant Dan like the character in *Forrest Gump*. She didn't know why I moved so funny but she guessed that it had to be a neurological condition, so she decided to call me

7

Neuro Dan instead. I really like that name. I don't know any other kitties with that name so that makes me even more unique.

There was one other kitty there that was about my age and she wasn't afraid of the funny way I walked or how my head bobbled around a bit. She was a pretty black cat named JuJu. She would snuggle with me in my pineapple and always stayed with me if any of the other cats tried to bully me. She even looked out for me when I ate. A lot of times, other cats would try to steal my food. KT did a good job of making sure I always got food but she had a lot of other kitties to care for as well, and couldn't be with me every minute. JuJu stayed with me though. She became my very best friend.

Days and days went by. And soon, the days turned into weeks. One day, KT told me she thought she knew the perfect person to adopt me. This lady was a big fan of KT's Facebook page for Easter the Extraordinarily Optimistic Kitten of Misfit Critter Farm. KT would put posts up of all the kitties she had who were ready for adoption. She would tell her fans all about their stories and their personalities. KT was really good at matching the right people with the right kitties. She told me that she just knew that a lady named Amanda was the one.

Amanda would comment on the stories KT would share about me all the time. KT even showed me her picture and I thought she looked really nice. KT said that Amanda and her husband, Eric, already had pets and they both worked full time jobs. They had talked long and hard about if they could manage to adopt and care for a special needs kitty and still manage everything else they had going on in their lives. KT was sad when Amanda said that she really wanted to, but felt like she had to say no. She just didn't think that she would have enough time to give me the attention that I would need.

Then, one day it happened. KT was very determined because she just knew that was supposed to be my home. She finally convinced Amanda to at least take me in and see if we could make it work. KT said I was going to be moving to Georgia and promised me that I would be very happy! Georgia is a very long way away from West Virginia. It's an eternity away for a little kitty like me who can't walk well. How was I going to be able to visit with JuJu?

I begged KT to convince her to take JuJu too. I gave her my sad eyes and tried so hard, but JuJu had to stay behind. KT said that there just wasn't enough room in their small two bedroom apartment to bring in another animal. She promised that she would take care of JuJu and that it would all work out. I couldn't help it and I was so sad about having to move away from my best friend ever that I cried.

That night, JuJu snuggled with me in my pineapple. We consoled each other and shared stories of how much fun we had. She told me she was so happy that I was going to have a Furever home and a family all of my own. I told her I was scared that the other pets they had would bully me like some of the other cats here. At least at Misfits I had JuJu to watch my back but she promised me I could take care of myself and that there was no way KT would send me anywhere if she was worried about that happening. She told me she overheard KT and Amanda talking about it. She said that Amanda was absolutely sure that nothing like that would happen and I shouldn't even worry. I couldn't help it though. I was really scared, but there was nothing I could do about it. Once again I was about to be out in the world alone.

The next morning came too fast. Before I knew it KT was kissing me goodbye and she was even crying a little. She told me I was going to be the happiest kitty in the world soon. JuJu went all the way to the door with me and KT had to pick her up to keep her from following me outside. JuJu told me to be brave and that we would see each other again, even if it was a long time away.

KT's friend, Ken, scooped me up and carried me towards the car that would take me to Georgia. Another thing about me is that I absolutely hate car rides! My condition makes it really hard for me to balance and I fall over every time there is a turn. Mum says that I'm not at all alone with this opinion and that most kitties don't like car rides. It was a very long ride with lots of turns and stops but I managed not to fall over too much.

I talked to Ken the entire ride. We knew each other pretty well because he hung out with me a lot at Misfit's. He even told me he would miss me too and that I was going to a great home. I tried to convince him to go back for JuJu, but he said he just couldn't do that. He promised I would make more friends and that I would like the other kitties at my new home. He said one of them was a boy ginger kitty like me and the other one was dark grey girl.

For such a long ride, it sure did feel like it went by quick talking with Ken and by the time we got there it was dark. He called my new family on his phone and all of a sudden a tall blond guy was waving at us. KT sent some of my favorite toys and things with me and the tall guy came over to help carry those while Ken carried me. We went on a short walk and down some stairs. Then we went inside. Everyone introduced themselves and Ken set me down on the floor.

It was a quiet, clean, place that had different smells but they smelled good. I did my Neuro hunker down sit where I make myself as flat as I can which puts me in the shape of that drag race car that KT said I looked like. A pretty blond lady was there and I recognized her from the pictures on the computer so I knew that was Amanda. She came to see me and she was so excited and her voice was so soothing and kind that I started to think I could really like her. She's my mum now so that's what I will call her from now on when I tell my story. Oh, and that tall blond guy he wound up being dad. I didn't know it then but I would wind up loving them more than anything else, even more than feathers!

I started to stand up and look around a little. I was hoping they wouldn't laugh at me and the way I moved. Mum got excited and sat down with me. She has such soft hands and gives the best gentle pets. Dad stayed back a bit and let me and mum meet. Ken kept giving me words of encouragement.

Then a really big orange cat came around the corner. Wow he was big, he had to be at least 15 pounds and all muscle. He looked like a warrior cat but he had very kind eyes and he came over to me. He said hi and that his name was Leroy. I was so nervous; I didn't want to have to worry about this big guy being a bully. As it turned out he was what mum calls a gentle giant and we sniffed noses and he gave me some space.

Then a small chubby grey cat came around the corner. She was very pretty and her grey coat had a neat shine to it. She came over and sniffed noses. She said her name was Amelia and wanted to know who I was. I told her I was Neuro Dan and she gave a tail twitch and walked away. I wasn't too sure about her, she wasn't near as friendly as Leroy was but I knew I was probably a surprise to her so I didn't worry too much.

I looked around and they have this great big giant sectional couch that goes down the entire length of the living room. It lines up with the hall way that goes to the front door and the hall to the other end of the apartment. Against the wall by that hallway on the other side of the couch was a huge cat tree. KT had some of those but I was always too afraid to try to check them out because the bully cats tended to play rough on it. I decided I would go investigate it and just as I started walking I heard something moving on the other side of the couch. All of a sudden, from around the end of the couch next to the cat tree appeared a black and white dog.

OH MY CAT they have a DOG!!!!!!

Chapter Two – The Cat Herder

A dog?? They have a dog?!?! Oh my CAT they have a DOG! And it was trotting right towards me with its great big wet black nose leading the way. Its bright brown eyes were looking right at me and it had this sloppy tongue hanging out of its mouth. It didn't even slow down as it went past everyone and came right up to me. It put that big wet nose right up to my face and gave me a couple of quick sniffs. I tried to stay still but it walked behind me and before I could even start to move, it sniffed my butt! That DOG just sniffed my BUTT! Oh no, I was not going to tolerate butt sniffing. That was just about the rudest thing I'd experienced. KT, what were you thinking? Why did you send me to a place that had a dog?!

I sprung up, legs shaking, head wobbling and as I mustered up my courage I did two things. First thing I did was poof. My fur stood on end and my tail popped up and looked like a giant orange Christmas tree. Then, with ears flat and a savage look on my face, I gave the scariest hiss I could muster. I even spit just a little bit. It didn't seem to scare the dog but it did look like it hurt its feelings which were just fine with me because it turned away from me and went to go check out Ken.

Ken did look a bit nervous at first but dad told him that the dog's name was Grace and she was friendly. He told him that she was half border collie and half blue heeler. She had grown up her entire life with cats. Dad said that she probably thought that she was a cat too. Grace sniffed Ken's hands and he pet her head. They seemed okay with each other. At least she didn't go and sniff his butt.

Ken asked dad how she behaved inside because he knew that border collies were working dogs and without a job, they tended to chew and destroy everything. Dad agreed with him and said that they found a way to give Grace a job that kept her working and busy all the time. He said she had a nick name and it was Cop Dog! What that meant was that she was basically a cat herder.

She was a very smart dog and was able to learn many commands. She even knew the names of all of the pets they ever had and learned hand signals. Her job was to make sure that everyone behaved in the house. If the cats started rough housing, running around too much or getting up where they weren't supposed to be, Cop Dog would go get them in line. Dad could even say one of the cats' names and point and she would jump into action. She would give a warning bark, chase them down the hall, put her nose up under their back side, lift the back legs up off the ground and wipe them out. Dad said with her black and white coloring she looked like an old police car in pursuit. She'd even pin them down against the wall. Dad called it the pit maneuver like what the police do when they are in car chases. He said once she had them on their back she would sniff and lick their bellies. He said she was very gentle with her mouth and had never hurt anyone.

I could not believe what I was hearing. KT, how could you send me to a place with a dog and not just any dog but one that was a professional cat herder? I looked at Grace and gave her another fierce hiss just for good measure. I certainly didn't want her rolling me over and licking my belly. Gentle or not I had no intention of having to try to clean dog drool off my belly.

Leroy and Amelia were still just sitting there, calm as could be. They were watching everyone and both looked really curious. Neither of them seemed a bit concerned that there was a dog wandering around sniffing everyone. As indignant as having my butt sniffed was I hoped that Grace was actually a nice dog. I would just have to be sure to establish some healthy boundaries with her right away.

Ken sat with me for a minute and talked to me but I knew he was saying goodbye. His eyes teared up, he told me to have a wonderful life and that he would miss me. Then he was out the door and gone. My eyes were teared up too. I was sad to say goodbye to Ken. I was getting really sad about having to say goodbye to so many friends.

I looked around and saw that everyone was staring at me. Mum started talking and sat down next to me. She reached out her hand and let me sniff her fingers and then gently pet my head. She told me my fur was very soft and felt nice to touch. She told me I had big beautiful eyes and that she loved my markings on my face. She was so genuine that it helped to chase away the tears from so many goodbyes. She got up and said they should just let me look around.

Dad knelt down to pet Grace and I could tell he was making sure she didn't bother me. I took advantage of it and stood up. Even though I was scared, I was also brave and I knew I couldn't just sit there. I turned around to see if there were any good places to hide. There was a kitchen table and chairs but that didn't look like a great spot. The kitchen was right there but I don't like kitchens very much. I had already seen what I wanted to go look at, so I decided to see if anyone had claimed the bottom ledge of that giant cat tree.

I started walking over to it and I was waiting to see if anyone was going to laugh at the way I was walking. Surprisingly, no one did. That made me feel a little better and after a few seconds; I made it to the cat tree. I stood in front of it and sniffed it. I got up on my back legs and looked up into the bottom ledge. I gave it a sniff and it didn't smell like it was used very often. That didn't surprise me because most cats like the top ledges better. I can't really get up that high, so I like the lowest ledges.

I sat back down and noticed that while I had been checking out the cat tree Amelia had hopped up on the edge of the couch and was looking down at me. Leroy had come up behind me but he was lying down and sprawled out, upside down, showing his big white belly. I appreciated that he was showing me he wasn't a threat. Amelia on the other hand had a funny look in her eye and was staring down at me. I couldn't tell what she was thinking. I would just keep an eye on her.

Having decided that the ledge was going to be my spot I figured I might as well snoop around a little bit. Mum made a comment about how my shoulder blades looked like they were rubbing together while I walked and after watching me for a few minutes, she sat down with me again and started feeling my shoulders. Mum and dad talked and dad sat down to pet me too. He had a soothing voice just like mum and his hands were kind as they pet my fur. Grace came over again, so I stood up, arched my back and gave her my mean look. Dad saw that and told Grace "no." He told her to go lay down. I was impressed! Grace turned around walked a few steps back, turned in a circle and laid down. She was watching closely but she just looked happy and curious.

Mum picked me up and said she was going to show me around so I would know where the important things like the food, water bowl and cat boxes were. Another thing that I really don't like is being held. I don't like it one bit. It makes me feel vulnerable and I always get scared about where I was going to be put down. It would be easy for someone to put me down somewhere that I might get stuck and wouldn't be able to walk out of. Another reason I don't like it is because of the way my shoulder blades touch each other. If I get held wrong, it hurts. It's hard to let humans know about things like that so I kick my back legs, wiggle and meow.

Mum seemed to understand right away and she managed to cradle me in a way that didn't hurt. She took me to all the important places and set me down next to the water bowl. I sniffed the food but still kept a close lookout for Leroy and Amelia. I learned from the other places I'd lived that food bowls tended to be a place where I would get attacked. Mum splashed the water in the bowl so I would see it and was a little worried when I didn't pay it any attention. I wasn't going to eat with everyone just standing there staring at me so I started to go back to the cat tree.

While I was making my way from the kitchen table along the walk way created by the couch, I heard what I thought might have been a horse

17

stampeding from all the way back towards the front door. I ducked down and Leroy went racing past me. He was very fast and had a long stride. He sounded like he was galloping. He jumped right past me and raced all the way down the hall towards a dark closet at the end. He stopped in front of the closet and turned around to give me a big grin. He twitched his tail and jumped, disappearing into the bedroom. A few seconds later he peaked around the corner and looked at me again. He was asking me if I'd like to play.

I never had any cat just come up and want to play after they saw me walk. That made me feel really good but I'd had a long day and was pretty stressed out. I mean there were all new people, new cats, a new place to have to learn my way around in and even a dog. I wasn't really in the mood to play at that moment so I finished my walk to the cat tree. I studied it for a minute and started the process of clawing my way up into it. It was a bit of a struggle for a second but then mum said she knew what I wanted, gave me a gentle boost and up I went. I sniffed around for a minute then made myself comfortable. The second ledge above the one I was in was a big tube with a hole in the top. It made for a great roof for the bottom ledge and that helped me feel pretty safe.

Mum and dad both took turns sitting down with me. They both talked to me and pet me. Then mum said they should just let me settle in. They went to the couch to sit down and watch TV. Grace came by one more time and sniffed me. I gave her another hiss. When dad heard me hiss, all he had to do was say

Grace's name and she left me alone. She then went and curled up by his feet.

I rested there quietly for the rest of the night. I was thinking about JuJu and I knew that she was thinking about me too. I knew she would be worried even though she was so happy for me. I couldn't think of a way to let her know that I was okay. I was pretty scared when Ken left, so I wasn't sure what he would say when he got back. I really didn't want her to worry about me. Letting her know I was okay was something I would have to figure out.

When mum went to bed that night she stopped and sat with me again for a minute. She really did know all the right spots to pet, like scritches' under the chin and on the nose. She was really good at giving those ears rubs too. She had a voice that I could just feel the love come from and I was already starting to like it when she would stop to see me like this. It didn't take long and I started to call that "getting my luvins."

Chapter Three – Surprises

Overnight, I learned that I didn't have to worry about Grace at night because she followed dad everywhere he went. When he went to bed, she went to bed and slept in there with him. She wouldn't come out until he did, which I liked a lot because there would be someone around just in case I had to do something more serious than hiss. Leroy and Amelia played a while at night and they both walked around the house like they were on patrol. They usually took turns doing that patrol. I thought it was odd but neither of them bothered me and it was a lot calmer and quieter than other places I'd lived at. They also slept in the bedroom with mum and dad.

In between their patrols I had snuck down because I had to do my business. Mum didn't know this yet but I can't use a normal litter box. I can't get up over the lip at the entrance and I sink into the litter and can't keep my balance. Then I fall and get stuck. I just went a little way into the living room to snoop around some and did my business there right in the middle of the floor. I snuck back up to my ledge before either Leroy or Amelia came back to do another patrol.

Amelia was the first one to come out after I did my business. She found it pretty quick. She tried to scratch at it to cover it up but I had already tried that and the carpet wasn't good for covering business. She seemed quite perplexed and it took a minute before she gave up and moved on. When Leroy came out he saw it, sniffed and just walked around it. He did that odd patrol and went back to bed. Because of all of the other animals at the other places I lived at, no one ever knew I had that issue. Everyone else always assumed that I was either using a box or that I was chased away by another cat. Mum and dad were about to learn that this was another challenge of my disability.

I was the first one awake that morning. Mum and dad came out at the same time with Grace walking right on dads heels. Dad went to the kitchen table and got a leash, hooked up Grace and they went outside. Mum stopped and greeted me with a "good morning." She then gave me some lovins. After that, she got up to go make some coffee. I knew what that was because KT and Ken had coffee in the mornings too. I recognized that this was a very important ritual for humans and that they were usually pretty clumsy and grumpy until the ritual was complete.

She came out of the kitchen with her coffee at the same time as dad came back inside with Grace. She then walked into the living room and saw the surprise I left her. She said "uh oh someone had an accident." She put down her coffee to go clean it up. Dad fed Grace. He then filled up the food bowls and water bowls for Leroy and Amelia. Dad thought that maybe I just forgot where the litter box was. Mum thought it was more likely too far away for me to get to.

Dad said he would take care of that and later that day he came back with a new litter box that he said was going to be just for me. He filled it up with litter, picked me up and set me in it. I knew what was going to happen and I didn't know what to do so I froze. My front feet always got stuck first and they did then too. When I tried to pull them out I sunk further, struggled and fell over. I kicked litter everywhere with my back

21

legs trying to get up. Mum reached in right away and pulled me out. She brushed me off and set me down on the floor. She then talked to me about how she could help me figure this out. She was so nice about it; she never once got mad. She was also really smart because she could tell that it was my disability that was the issue and she already knew that litter wasn't going to work.

Mum always seemed to know what to do and dad always took her advice anytime any of us needed anything vet, medicine or food related. Mum had been a veterinary technician for many years and had taken many college classes on medical stuff over the years. She also had a great intuition and it was very rare when she couldn't tell us what was wrong or what we needed. This time she told dad we would have to figure out something else to put in the litter box other than litter.

She got in touch with KT and asked her what they used for me. KT said that I never had that issue there, but that she sometimes used pellets. That's when mum realized that nobody had ever figured out I had a problem with doing my business. She told dad to go get some newspapers and that they would try to shred them up to see if I could keep my balance on them.

Dad got back with a newspaper. They cut it up into strips and put it in the box. I watched them from my ledge. I was curious to see if this would work. I didn't have to go but mum set me down in the box to see how I would do. I was excited but I was nervous too. I wasn't too nervous because I didn't actually need to go so I wasn't worried about falling in a surprise and getting messy. The newspaper strips were difficult for me to walk on. You see, when I walk I don't actually walk just on the pads of my front feet. I actually walk on my front legs from the elbows all the way to my feet. Sometimes when I'm determined to get somewhere and I'm moving quickly, I get more up on my ankles, but it's not easy. With the newspaper, I slid around a bit. My front feet couldn't hold any traction. My back legs would slip and I'd lose my balance again but I didn't actually fall down.

Mum said she wasn't sure if that would work but it would be worth a try. She left me in there to get some practice with it and to see if I would use it. I really didn't have to go. I wasn't having any fun and didn't think practicing would help, so I decided to try to get out. When I tried to get my front feet over the exit area my back legs would slip on the newspaper. Then I fell and hit my chin on the edge of the box. I tried again. This time I tried to jump and it went really bad. I wound up falling down and that made mum jump up and come rescue me again. This was getting embarrassing.

She put me back on my ledge and sat next to me to give me lovins again. She and dad talked and she said that a litter box might not work because I couldn't get in or out of it without possibly getting hurt and even getting myself messy. Dad said that he had an idea. He went into a closet and came out with a saw. He sat down on the floor and started sawing at the front of the cat box. Mum asked him what he was doing and dad said he was removing the front so I could just walk in and out.

Mum and I both thought that was a great idea and when he was done mum put me back on the floor in front of the litter box. She kept pushing on my rear until I walked in. This time the litter box was much easier to walk into. I didn't have to try to climb or anything. I still slid around on the paper but when I went to leave I tried to climb out the back side of it. Mum picked me up and turned me around and I walked out the front. Mum told dad he did a really good job and everyone hoped that would help me overcome the challenge.

Later that day a visitor came to the house. That was when I learned that Grace didn't like it when people knocked on the door. Anytime someone knocked on the door she would jump up, start barking and run in front of the door. The more they would knock the more she would bark. When mum or dad tried to open the door she would try to push past them and to the front of the door to see who was there. I didn't think she sounded like she was trying to make friends either. Well, this time, as soon as the door opened the barking stopped and her tail started wagging really fast.

Two ladies came in; one of them was really small and really old with grey hair and lots of wrinkles. She walked with a cane and moved pretty slow. The other one I got introduced to right away. Mum brought her over to the cat tree and introduced me to her. As it would turn out, this lady was mum's mum and I came to love her dearly. I decided I would call her gramma. Well, the old lady with the cane was gramma's mum and I would come to love her too. I called her gramma great. They were both really nice and they sure did seem to like me quite a lot.

Mum set me on the floor so they could see how I walked. I wasn't really sure about that. I really just wanted to be back on my ledge on the cat tree, so I started walking that way. Gramma great said I was precious. She said she brought me some treats. Well, I already knew what that word meant, so I stopped going to my ledge and turned to look at her. Sure enough, she had a bag of treats called Temptations. She had a fish flavor, which smelled really good. She was very gentle when she held it between two fingers and handed it to me.

It was delicious and I got as many of them as I could before they left. They also made sure Leroy and Amelia had some treats too. Gramma great even brought a special treat for Grace that she called a chew bone. Grace would sit and beg for it. When she got it, she tossed it in the air and pounced on it before she started chewing it up. I was paying pretty close attention to that bag of treats and I noticed that mum put them in the bottom drawer of her desk.

The rest of the day was pretty quiet. I was very surprised to see that Grace really didn't bother me much at all. She would stop and sniff now and then while she walked by but at least she didn't try to sniff my butt. Since she was being nice I stopped hissing at her when she got close to me.

Later that night mum noticed that I hadn't eaten any of the food that she had put on the ledge. She asked dad if he had seen me drink any water. Dad told her he didn't. Mum got worried came over to sit down and talk to me again. She asked me why I wasn't hungry and said that I had to drink or I'd get sick. She picked me up and took me over to the water bowl and set me down in front of it. She splashed the water a little bit and waited to see if I would drink.

I was very thirsty but drinking was extremely difficult for me. I did try, but one of the effects of my disability is that I struggle to hold my head steady depending on how my neck is angled and how my shoulders are set. When I tried to drink, my shoulder blades rubbed together and my head bobbed up and down. This wasn't something that bothered me much in the past, but the last few weeks it had been getting worse. Nobody ever noticed it until mum watched me try to drink and my whole face went straight into the water bowl and under up to my eyes. I pulled my head out and coughed. I tried again and got a little drink, but it happened again. I was very frustrated, so I turned around and looked at my ledge.

Mum was upset and said I had to get fluids. She said that she would have to figure something out. She talked it over with dad for a long time and I could tell they were both worried. Mum sent dad out to the store and when he came back she went into the kitchen. Then I heard the sound of the lid of a can being peeled off. Mum was doing something with a plate and I heard her talking to dad about adding more water.

When she came back out of the kitchen she was carrying a plate and had a spoon. She sat down on the floor next to my ledge and talked to me about trying to eat something different. She had a plate of pate-style wet food and she had mixed it up with some water. She piled it up on the plate and put it next to me. I looked at it and I had to admit that it smelled really good. After a few sniffs I realized I was very

26

hungry too, so I tried a little bite. It was good and I started eating. Mum kept piling it up with the spoon so it looked like a little mountain of food. I'd bite off the top of the mountain and she used her spoon to put another mountain top back on it. It felt really good to get the wet food and I started to purr. That was the first time mum ever heard me purr and for some reason it made her really happy. The great big smile on her face made me happy too.

That was my first full day in my Furever home. I was surprised that I was already starting to like it and I was really happy how smart mum was. I thought that just maybe KT was right and this might have been a good idea.

Chapter Four – Sink Baths

The next day when mum woke up she sat down to say hi to me before she even went to get her coffee. She petted me for a second, then got a worried look on her face and said "oh no what happened." Well, what happened was I used that litter box last night and things didn't exactly go the way we had all hoped. My surprise didn't cover very well with the paper and I couldn't get out of the back of the box. By the time I managed to get out, I was covered in "surprise" from my chest all the way down to my back legs.

Mum called out for dad. When he came out of the bedroom, she told him what had happened and said that they were going to have to give me a bath. He got a surprised look on his face and I got a scared look on mine. A bath is just about the absolute last thing any cat wants to hear anyone say that they are going to have to get. Most kitties would have jumped and ran as soon as they heard that but I couldn't do much about it. Dad wanted to know just exactly how they were going to do that. Mum told him to go get a couple of towels, some baby shampoo and to meet her at the kitchen sink.

I was trying to plot my escape. I was hoping mum would get up and turn her back for just a minute. I could do a jump off my ledge, face plant on the carpet and scramble as fast as I could to anywhere that looked like a good hiding spot. I had gone on a floor adventure last night and I found a couple of places that looked like they would make for good places to disappear.

Well, mum didn't turn her back. Once dad got to the sink with the supplies she told him fill one half of the sink a quarter way up with warm water and to let her know when he was done. When he finished, she gently scooped me up and into the kitchen I went. This was the very last time I ever got carried into the kitchen without kicking and crying in my most pathetic as possible meow.

I saw that mum was about to set me in the water so I did what any proper cat would do and I kicked all my legs out to the side as far as I could, scratched and clawed at anything and everything I could to try to not get in that water. Mum seemed to expect that I was going to do that and she had dad help her out. When my tail hit the water I even tried my mournful howl meows which sometimes makes people feel so bad that they just stop. Mum didn't stop though and I found myself plopped into the sink, soaking in water.

She scrubbed and scrubbed and then drained the water and got out the sink sprayer. She got the water warm and put the nozzle really close to my belly and started spraying me down. I kept up my protests with mournful meows and leg kicks. I managed to get both of them pretty wet but even that didn't work to get them to stop. The entire ordeal felt like it took hours but mum said it was over in about 15 minutes.

When she was done she lifted me in the air under my shoulders, had dad wring me out and try to get me as dry as possible. Then she had him towel dry me and when she said it was good enough, she grabbed the second towel and wrapped me up in it. She held me close to her chest and took me to her desk chair. She talked to me and rocked me until I started calming down. She used the towel to pat me dry and when she felt I was as dry as she could get me she put me back on my ledge.

One of the worst parts for any cat when it comes to a sink bath is how long it takes to get the fur right again. I spent the rest of the day grooming myself but because of my condition I had a difficult time getting it right. Mum noticed and got out her cat grooming brush. She sat with me and helped me get myself back together again.

Dad was brainstorming, trying to come up with another way to take care of my litter box issues. None of us enjoyed getting that sink bath. He went back out to the store and when he came back he had puppy training pads. I wasn't exactly sure what he was going to do with that. He and mum talked and dad went back to the closet. He came back with the saw again. He sawed the other end of the cat box off and told me that now I could just walk in and walk out. No more trying to climb or turn around and maybe that would do it. Then he folded the pee pad into squares and put in the cat box. It was a pretty good fit with no edges for me to trip over.

Mum picked me up and set me in front of the box. I gave it a skeptical look because I'm not a dog, but mum gave me a gentle nudge from behind and I went ahead and walked in. Again, I didn't have to go, so I stopped for a moment to sniff it. I hadn't smelled that thing before but it didn't stink so I thought it was okay. It felt really weird on my feet and every now and then I'd have a nail snag on it and that would make it come up with my foot. I'd have to do that foot shake like when you step in water to get it off. I didn't care for that part because it tickled a little. I walked right out of it with no trouble at all.

Dad was happy but mum was a bit skeptical. She agreed they would give it a try and they left it next to the cat tree. Mum helped me back up to my ledge and I got a good dinner that night. The wet food was really doing the trick and was keeping me hydrated. That made both me and mum happy.

The new cat box idea didn't work as well as dad hoped it would. That night I jumped down, fell on my face again and went to use the box. I got in and did my business okay, but kitties just can't help but scratch and cover. It's just what we do. Well when I tried to be a decent, polite kitty and cover my surprise, the pad got caught on my front foot and back foot. It got that surprise all over the side of the litter box and all over the side of my tail. I managed to escape the box but dragged the pad out with me.

I was frustrated. I didn't know what I was going to do. I knew the only way this was going to work was if I could just go walk somewhere like the floor, do my business, scratch for a minute and walk away. I was worried they would get frustrated with the situation soon. I didn't know if they would be willing to put up with this part of my condition. I was worried that after a few days of this that they just wouldn't want me.

I went on a little floor adventure and started checking out the rest of the living room. Leroy came out on one of his odd patrols and saw the state of my litter box but it didn't seem to bother him one bit. He came up to me while I was between the coffee table and the couch and we sniffed noses. He was a big guy

31

but he really was quite friendly. He told me not to worry, that I was in the right place and gave me a couple grooming licks on my forehead. He then went back about his patrol. I decided I'd get back up on my perch before Amelia got up to go on her patrol.

Amelia wasn't being mean to me but she was always staying somewhere higher where she could look down on everything. She just had this look in her eyes like she was trying to decide if she was going to like me or not. I was kind of getting the feeling that we weren't going to be friends like I was with JuJu but I thought maybe I could be good friends with Leroy.

I climbed back up onto my ledge and waited for the morning to come. Mum had been talking to dad about both of them having to work tomorrow. That meant tomorrow I would be on my own. I guess I would find out if Grace was going to be a problem or not. I hoped they would remember to feed me. They had been making sure I ate twice a day; once in the morning and once in the evening. They were doing a good job with my food and I really appreciated it. I also wondered if a dirty tail was going to mean another sink bath. I really didn't want another sink bath.

I got lucky and didn't end up getting a bath that morning. Mum was able to wash it off with warm water, a wash cloth and a bunch of scrubbing. I didn't complain at all and it didn't take her too long to get the mess all cleaned up.

She made my breakfast and dad took Grace out for her morning ritual. When he came back in, they talked while I was eating. It was going to be dads turn to feed me when he got home because mum was going to be out later. I felt better knowing that they were getting my meals planned out. I didn't want to sit there hungry all day. Plus, I was going to need my energy if I decided to go do some exploring while they were gone.

Dad left for work and mum sat and gave me luvins for a while. Leroy and Amelia had both come over and were begging for some of my food while I was eating. Mum gave them each a small bite and what I didn't finish she put up on the table next to their food bowl for them to finish it off. When I first got there, I only weighed about four pounds, so it didn't take a whole lot to fill me up; at least not in the beginning.

Once mum left I waited to see what everyone did while they were alone. Grace walked by, gave me a friendly sniff and laid down in the middle of the living room. I thought it looked like she put herself where she had a good view of the glass door in the living room and the hallway next to where I was.

From the spot on my ledge, I had a terrific view of the entire house. I could see all the way down the hall to the front door. I could see the glass door in the living room; almost the entire living room and I could peak around the corner and look down towards the bedroom and that closet at the other end. Leroy wandered into the second bedroom by the front door. Amelia crawled up into the chair at dad's desk in the living room next to the glass door.

I waited a while, but no one did anything at all. It was actually very quiet. I was not used to someplace where it was so calm and quiet. I was used to staying alert and watching for bullies or trying to sneak to the food bowl without getting run off. It was so calm and quiet I had no idea what to do.

I got a sudden urge to tell JuJu that I really thought I was going to be okay. I was starting to work on an idea that would allow JuJu to check up on me even though she was so far away. I figured that since everyone else was taking a nap, I would do the same thing and let that new idea roll around in my mind. As I dozed off, I thought that this really was a wonderfully quiet place. I wondered if this is what it was like for all the other kitties that already had their Furever homes and didn't live in a shelter or rescue.

Chapter Five – Amelia

When I woke up Amelia was right in front of me! She was standing on her back legs with her front paws on my ledge and she was giving me this snarky, glaring look. I shook my head to make sure she was really there and I was not dreaming. Then I gave her my wide eyed no blinking stare back to let her know I wasn't interested in her or whatever it was she wanted. Her ears went flat and she gave me one long ugly hiss. I wasn't going to take that kind of attitude lying down so I started to get up and she did two fast double hisses and a guttural growl. This was what I was hoping wouldn't happen when mum and dad left me alone. I was used to that from some of the bully cats at Misfit's and I wasn't about to put up with it here.

I was about to establish some serious boundaries with her right then when something remarkable happened. Grace, who had been lying in the middle of the living room snoozing, gave one sleepy muffled woof then sprung to her feet. She must have known exactly where the hiss had come from and who had done it because she looked right at Amelia, gave a loud bark and charged. Amelia's yellow eyes went wide and she used her cat reflexes to spin towards the bedroom but Grace had covered the distance between the middle of the living room and the cat tree incredibly quickly. In two steps she was already full speed ahead and Amelia didn't stand a chance.

Amelia was fast too though. She was all but tearing bits of carpet up with her back legs as she

tried to escape. It wasn't enough. Grace caught her
before she got three steps. That big black shiny nose
was thrusted between Amelia's back legs and with a
flip of her head; Grace tossed her up against the wall.
Amelia rolled once before she hit the wall and tried to
get her feet under her again, but Grace was really
good at this. She nosed her in the middle of her roll
which caused Amelia to be four feet in the air when
she made contact with the wall. Grace used her nose
to spin her again then pinned her to the floor then
started, licking and drooling on her belly.

Amelia made terrible hissing and growling noises
but Grace wouldn't have any of it. She did a couple of
muffled, quick popcorn barks right into her belly.
Amelia's eyes went wide in desperation and she
finally managed to squirm free. She leapt up onto the
couch, jumped across to the kitchen counter and kept
on going. I'm not sure where she went in there but
she stayed there for at least an hour and when she
came out she wouldn't even look at me. She must
have been really embarrassed.

Once Grace had finished with Amelia she turned
around and walked over to me. Her tail was up and
wagging she looked incredibly proud of herself. She
stood in front of me for a minute and gave me a
couple of sniffs on the head. When she decided I was
okay, she went back to her napping spot in the middle
of the living room. She turned around three times
gave a big sigh then curled up and took another nap.

Now I understood what dad meant about her not
putting up with any horse play or rough housing. If
this was her job she sure was good at it. She had
saved me an awful lot of aggravation. Except for the

whole butt sniffing thing, I was starting to like Grace. I didn't know it right then, but within a few weeks, I figured out that Grace became my bodyguard. She was a secret weapon to help keep me safe but I'll share more about that later.

Dad got home later that evening. He put down his work things and came over and sat down with me for a minute. He gave me luvins and then went into the kitchen. I heard the sound of a can lid being peeled off again. That was one of my all-time favorite sounds because it meant that I was about to get food. When I heard that sound I'd stand up stretch my back then sit down and wait impatiently. He came out in a few minutes and sat down to feed me.

Mum got home right after he finished. She came right over to my ledge to greet me. I had gotten a lot of food on my face, so she got food all over her fingers when she gave me luvins but she didn't seem to mind. She got up to get a towel and helped me get myself cleaned up. She talked with dad for a little while before picking me up to take me to the living room. She then sat on the floor right next to me.

She got a couple of toys down from the top of the cat tree. I didn't know she kept toys up there but I was learning. She got a toy mouse, a ball with a jingly thing in it and a stick with a string with a ball on the end of it. She played with me for a while and I had fun but it was hard for me to play like normal cats. Mum wasn't sure what else to do with me so she decided to leave me in front of the litter box just in case I needed to use it.

Mum and dad sat down together on the couch to watch TV. Amelia hopped up on the couch with them and she got some luvins. I decided not to tell on Amelia because Grace took care of it and I was hoping she was just nervous because I was new. Grace took up her usual position in front of dad's feet and chewed on one of her bones.

I decided to listen to them talk because I had been thinking of my plan to find a way for JuJu to check up on me. Every time I heard mum or dad mention Facebook I would stand up. Sometimes I would look at them and sometimes I would just turn around, but I was trying really hard to give clues. I have to admit they weren't really getting any of my subtle cues. I was always a very persistent boy so I just kept on trying every night.

That night I had another issue with the litter box and in the morning I got another sink bath; although it wasn't nearly as bad as the first one. I didn't know it then but I would get quite a few of those over the next couple of weeks. Mum and dad tried idea after idea to find a way to solve the riddle of my business but I just couldn't manage to navigate anything they tried. I was still worried that they were getting frustrated.

Amelia became much more careful with how she expressed herself when mum and dad weren't home. She tried to hiss at me from the arm of the couch once. I guess she thought that Grace wouldn't be able to bother her up there, but she was wrong. Grace jumped right up on the couch, knocked her off and jumped down after her. She got Amelia with her pit maneuver again, and much to Amelia's chagrin, it resulted in another belly full of dog drool.

Amelia and Grace had a strange relationship that took me a while to figure out. The first time I saw

Amelia loving on Grace really took me by surprise. Grace had been sitting in front of the glass door, looking outside, when Amelia walked right up to her and started mushing all over her. She mushed her way all the way up to her head. Grace put her head on her paws and Amelia gave Grace grooming kisses on the top of her head for several minutes while she purred up a storm.

Amelia did this with Grace a lot. She really loved that dog, which made me have to reevaluate how I felt about Amelia. She wasn't just this sassy, mean girl cat after all. She was actually very sweet and didn't seem to hold any hard feelings about all those times Grace gave her the pit maneuver and a wet belly.

Amelia and Leroy were funny to watch. They would get the zoomies and chase each other around the house all the time. I loved to watch them have the zoomies. I would get excited, pop up on my ledge and make loud goose-honk noises at them when they ran by.

Amelia would usually forget she was playing and start hissing. Leroy didn't seem to care about the hissing one bit. He'd just shrug his shoulders and go find something else to do. At least that's what he would do most of the time. Sometimes, he wouldn't be done playing yet, or maybe he just wanted a little danger in his life, but he'd keep playing with her while she told him she was done. He was really brave because he'd just keep getting closer and closer. She would hiss time and again and he'd just slow-walk up to her until they got into a tense standoff that wouldn't end until one of them, usually Amelia, pounced on the other.

Amelia really held her own well against big old Leroy. Leroy was muscle big and Amelia was chubby big, but she sure knew how to use that weight to her advantage. She could crouch low, pounce up under Leroy, grab him by the head with all fours and flip him to the ground. That kind of play time usually got Grace involved pretty quickly and they'd both take off as fast as they could. It was a toss-up as to who Grace would catch but one of them usually got the pit maneuver. When Grace was after more than one suspect she gave a lot more than one warning bark, she'd make a racket that would sometimes get mum and dad to fuss at her and tell her to be quiet. She would also stay alert for whichever one she didn't get and if they came back out before she dozed off or got distracted by her bone, she'd usually get them too.

Leroy would ask me to play all the time. I tried to explain to him that I couldn't do the zoomies like other kitties, but he didn't understand. It was very sweet of him to never take it personally and he always came back to ask over and over again. Sometimes, I thought he was pretty smart and other times, I wondered how he managed to keep himself alive. I found out that mum and dad named him Leroy after a cartoon character from a video game named Leroy Jenkins. That Leroy was famous for having gotten bored and charging blindly into a room full of dragons screaming his name as a battle cry. All of his team mates who were planning the attack ran in behind him to try to save the day. They all got eaten by the dragons and had to start the game over.

Leroy could be just like that. He wouldn't always look before he leapt. He'd get the zoomies out of nowhere and run into dads legs all the time. He would also get the zoomies and jump over Grace. That always made her go cop dog, which would result in Leroy getting the pit maneuver and a belly covered in drool. He could be very clumsy, but I think it was really that he didn't know how big he was and had a hard time maneuvering his own body. He was always knocking things off tables and counters. Sometimes, he would even fall off the table or misjudge a jump and land ugly.

Mum and dad managed to settle into a routine with taking care of me. Dad usually had Saturday and Sunday off and mum usually had Monday off as well as time in the mornings to feed me. Dad would feed me on the weekends and then he gave me my dinners and mum would feed me on Monday and most mornings. I liked that a lot because I got to spend lots of time with both of them. It usually took from a half hour to forty five minutes for them to feed me.

Each night they did their chores or worked on their computers, but every night they tried to be done with work by eight o clock. Then they would go sit together on the couch and talk and watch T.V. They'd sit there until about ten o'clock. Then mum would declare it bed time and go to sleep. Sometimes dad would stay up a little later. They both always stopped on their way to bed to give me luvins and tell me goodnight before disappearing into the bedroom.

I stayed on my ledge most of the time, but I really enjoyed listening to them talk. I enjoyed the calm and quiet, and I loved it when they would stop to give me luvins. One day, dad told mum that he was worried that all I did was stay on the ledge. He said he was worried I was bored and miserable. He decided that if I was going to stay on the ledge, he'd try to bring some of the fun to me. He figured out a way to set up a series of toys tied to bouncy strings and hung them from different parts of the cat tree. He said that he noticed that I always played with the small mice that had big feathers for tails and so he set up a bunch of toys with feathers. At that point, he had no idea just how much I really loved feathers.

I played hard with those toys he set up for me and sometimes; Leroy would play with them with me. We finally found a way to play together. Amelia played with them a little, but she was more interested in whatever was all the way at the top of the tree. I was finally starting to relax and enjoy myself. Mum even said that I was starting to look like I was smiling and boy she was right. I really was.

Chapter Six – Facebook

Neuro Dan - Feather Dan
February 24, 2015 ·

Hi all my friends. I am Neuro Dan. I have been dealt a rough hand in life. I was rescued by Misfit Critters Farm from a hoarding situation. Mom says I am a precious little boy but I have a lot of issues. I can't walk right and live in a lot of pain. It does not stop me though. I love my humans and sing for them all the time. I also love for my belly to be rubbed. Oh and the toy birds that chirp send me into a frenzy!

My subtle attempts at dropping hints with mum finally worked. One afternoon when she managed to get a day off she sat down and made me my very own Facebook page. I knew without a doubt that KT would be sure to like my page. I also knew she'd be curious to see how I was doing and check on me all the time. That meant that JuJu was sure to hear KT talk about it and then she'd be able to jump up to take a peek.

I was so happy that I stood up and did a happy dance. Mum saw me doing my happy dance so she came to get me off my ledge. She took me over to the couch, set me down and sat with me. She asked me what I thought about having my very own page and played with me for a bit. She must have been listening to dad, because she had a toy that was full of feathers. She waited until I was really focused on it, and then snuck the picture. That picture would become my first official Facebook picture to go with my first official Facebook post. None of us had any idea what an incredible journey we would go on with that page.

Oops... I did it again. I got so excited thinking about getting my Facebook page so JuJu could see me that I completely forgot about the trip to the vet that I had to go on right before that happened. It's easy for me to forget about those nasty appointments because I really hated it when I had to go. Mum was determined to find out what was wrong with me. She said if we could get a diagnosis, we might be able to find something or someway to help me live a more fun life filled with normal kitty adventures. I liked the idea but I didn't like what the process would entail.

Trips to the vets were filled with all of my don't likes. They start by getting picked up; don't like. Then I get put into a carrier; don't like. Then I have to go on a car ride; big don't like. Then we would sit in a room with a lot of other animals and there were usually dogs that won't shut up; big don't like. Then I would get carried to the exam room and set down on a cold table that was so smooth I couldn't get any traction. That would make me slip, fall over and hurt my shoulder blades; huge don't like. Then there were all the things that they do to kitties at the vet; do not like.

On that particular trip I learned about my absolute, number one don't-like of some of the trips to the vets. Sometimes you don't get to go home with mum and dad. On that particular trip, the vet said something about wanting to keep me overnight. They gave me some pain medicine to see if it would help improve my walking. They thought maybe it was but the vet wanted to keep me overnight to see if I progressed any further.

When she said that, I looked at mum. I could tell mum wasn't happy at all. She asked all kinds of questions about what they would feed me, if she could leave a special blanket that I liked to lay on and some toys to play with. She said she would even go get me my food and feed me to help them out. Mum gave me some pretty hard luvins before she left. I thought I might have even seen a tear in her eye as she walked out the door.

The vet was actually very nice and gentle but she wasn't mum or dad. I wished they could have left Grace with me. I never thought I'd wish a dog would have been with me but Grace had become a great bodyguard. I was scared and I missed the safe feeling I had when she was around. I would probably even tolerate a butt sniff if she could just spend the night with me.

They really didn't do a whole lot with me. Every hour they would come by and see if they could get me to walk a little but when I'm scared I just sit there and don't move. I got medicine now and then, but other

45

than that, not much at all happened. They gave me some food and they even gave me wet food but they just put it in my cage. Mum and dad would have sat down with me to help me eat and talked to me. There were cats meowing and howling and dogs barking. I curled up on the blankets mum left for me, buried my head down into my tummy and just waited for the morning.

The next day was pretty much a repeat of the previous evening. I did eat a little of the wet food they brought me in the morning but I made a huge mess of my chin. I refused to use the cat box because I didn't want to have a sink bath. Well, that made them think that maybe I was dehydrated so they stuck me with a needle to give me fluids.

Shortly after lunch they came to get me and took me back to an exam room. When they opened the door I saw my mum! I was so excited that I got a huge case of the wiggles because I wanted to get to her. She smiled said my name and got right up. They set me on the exam table and she started petting me and talking to me. I sang for her, purring so loud that I made a trilling noise. That got mum all kinds of happy. She talked to the vet and I was relieved when I heard them say I could go back home. They didn't know what to do with me and said they weren't equipped to make a diagnosis. The vet told mum she could arrange an appointment at Auburn University and the specialists there would have the best chance at figuring me out.

Mum talked to me the entire drive home which made the drive not so bad, so I talked right back to her. I didn't mind the drives home nearly as much as the drives there. I was pretty hungry and was looking forward to mum feeding me supper. I had a little gas on the way home too which made mum make some funny faces. Every now and then, the window would come down to air out the car too.

When mum brought me home, the first thing she did was put me in my litter box. Whew was I grateful because I really had to take care of business. She stood beside me and as soon as I was done, she scooped me up to set me on the floor while she cleaned up my surprise. While she was doing that everyone came over to see me.

I learned that when you go to the vet, you come back with strange smells on you. Grace was the first one get to me. She gave me lots of big dog sniffs, which was more than she'd ever sniffed me before. At least she was polite and didn't sniff my butt again. Amelia came up beside Grace but when she got close enough to me she gave me a big hiss and ran off. Grace didn't chase her this time. She kept sniffing me so I knew I must smell funny. Leroy came over and sniffed me with his whole mouth wide open. Then he got some strange, goofy look in his eyes and walked away.

Mum set me back on my ledge and I was so happy to be home that I got frisky. I played hard with those toys dad had hung on the tree for me. Leroy can never stay away from a good round of play time, so it didn't take him long to come over to play with me.

When dad got, home he fed me my supper while mum did work on her computer. I told him how much I don't like the vet and he agreed that going to the human vet wasn't usually very fun either. When I finished eating, he got a bunch of toys off of the cat tree, took a couple apart and made me a big funny looking feather toy. He tied it to a string and played with me for a while. Amelia even decided that the toy was fun so she played too. She doesn't usually play with me but every now and then even Amelia can't resist a good feather toy.

When mum and dad sat down on the couch that night, they talked about this place called Auburn. Apparently there is a really good veterinary program there and they have specialists in everything that they teach. I guess I'm so special that they thought they could learn from me, so they let mum make an appointment with the neurologists. Mum said it was about three weeks away and she wanted dad to go with us this time. Dad agreed that he wanted to be there so they set the date. It sounded like a really long way away which would mean a really long car ride. Ugh, I just put it out of my mind because it wasn't going to do me any good to worry about it. Plus, I had that new feather toy dad made that I just couldn't quit chomping on.

Neuro Dan - Feather Dan

March 25, 2015 ·

Hi all, Neuro Dan here. Mum and dad really really want to help me be able to walk and be a more normal kitty. They have already put a lot of resources into getting me to this point. Now they just need a little help getting me the rest of the way. It is going to cost a lot of money to get all my tests done. Auburn University is willing to do it, but they estimated the cost to be $2,000. If you have a spare dollar or two, would you mind donating to help me? If you can afford it, please go to PayPal and donate .... If you can't donate, please send me prayers and love. I love all my friends! - Neuro Dan

During those three weeks I had two other follow-up trips to the vet. Fortunately I didn't have to spend the night again and got to go home with mum each time. Mum got in the habit of taking someone else with her when she went. The next trip she took gramma and the one after that she took dad. That let her ride and let me sit on her lap during the drive. I liked that a whole bunch. It made it so I didn't have to worry about losing my balance or being rolled around. Plus, mum would give me luvins and talk to me during the rides.

Each trip home was the same too. Mum would first set me in my litter box, and then onto the floor in the living room. Grace would give me lots of curious sniffs. Amelia would get close to me, hiss and run off. Leroy would sniff me until his jaw hung open and that weird, silly look would come over his face. He would then wander off somewhere. I don't know where he wandered off to or what he did, but he acted like he'd been into the catnip. I didn't take Amelia's hisses personally, I just rolled my eyes.

I had been getting more and more playful too. Mum said that I was starting to get a little belly on me and that I was looking much better with the extra weight on. I still only weighed about five pounds so mum said she wanted to see me keep eating well.

One morning mum and dad both had to go to work super early. That meant mum had to feed me much sooner than I was used to. I didn't much care for that, I was still sleepy and wasn't really hungry. I ate about two bites and turned away to go back to sleep. Mum was concerned because she knew she would feel terrible if I had to sit there hungry all day. Neither of them was going to be home until after dark. It was issues like this that she had been concerned about in the beginning and why she had originally told KT she couldn't take me. Well she had fallen in love with me so I wasn't worried. I knew she'd figure something out and if she didn't, I would just have to be hungry. It wasn't the end of the world.

Mum got an idea, so she called gramma on the phone. They talked for a while and mum told me to be good for gramma before she hurried out the door. I had no idea what she was talking about so I went back to sleep. Around lunch time, I heard a key in the front door. Grace barked and ran to the door. Then her tail started wagging and gramma and gramma-great came inside. Gramma-great shuffled over to me to say hello. Gramma was on the phone with mum and mum was talking her through how to make my food.

Gramma came over to sit down with me and started feeding me. I loved it! I was getting to have a lunch date with gramma. Over the years I would have many lunch dates with gramma and I loved every single one of them. Gramma great always made sure everyone got lots of treats before they left. I thought this was wonderful. Not only did I get my food but we all got treats too. Grace even got a new chew bone which made her extra happy.

The time for my trip to Auburn came very quickly. One morning, mum and dad got me up really early. I knew I was going somewhere because mum had my cat carrier out. She bought me a nice one that wasn't just a hard, plastic box. It had lots of places to peak out, different parts that she could open to pet me and a very comfortable sleeping mat. She even put a couple of my favorite snuggling blankets in there along with a few of my feather toys.

Unless she had to take me to the vet on her own, mum only used it to get me from the car into the vet's offices. When she was able to, she would hold me during all of our car rides and this was going to be one really long one. Mum said it would take about three hours just to get there and that this was going to be an all-day event. It was a very pretty day. It was sunny and even though it was March it wasn't very cold out.

Mum gave dad grief for a good part of the drive. She would fuss at him if he took a turn too fast or stopped too abruptly. She was determined that I was going to have a comfortable ride. Plus, every time I got a little off balance my claws would come out and since I was being held by mum, she kept getting scratched.

When we got there, mum put me back in my carrier and zipped it up tight. The parking lot was full and there were other people walking around; some of them with dogs. Mum told me not to worry that all of the other animals were there because they needed help too and none of them would bother me.

We went inside and got checked in. Mum unzipped one of the flaps in my carrier and let me peak out. The ladies at the reception desk were very sweet and said hi to me. They said I was a cutie. We then went back to the waiting area. This place was much different than the other vets offices I'd been to. It was huge and I could tell it was someplace special. There were a couple of other people in the waiting area. One person must have been waiting for their fur-baby to

54

come out because they were alone and there was couple sitting a little way down who had a beagle dog in their lap. The dog must not have been feeling well because it just laid there and looked a little sad.

Mum opened up my carrier and turned it so she and dad could see in. They took turns petting me and reading some papers the receptionists had given them. One of the vets came out and talked to mum for a little while and when she left she said it would only be a few more minutes. She let us know what door we would be going to so we'd know where to go. I was getting nervous because I knew I was about to get poked and prodded again.

Soon, the door opened up and in we went. Mum set me on the table and opened up the carrier. The vet introduced herself to mum and dad and they talked for a minute. Mum got me out of my carrier and dad put it on the chairs behind them. She sat me on the exam table, which was cold and slippery. I slid all over the place until I could finally just get myself hunkered down. The vet had a soft touch and a kind voice. She picked me up and checked me out while mum explained everything that she could about me. The vet paid extra attention to how my shoulder blades touched. She then sat me back on the table to see if I would stand up so she could see me better.

I didn't want any part of it so I just hunkered down again. Each time she tried to get me to stand up I would sit right back down. She realized that I couldn't stand on the table so she asked everyone to sit down on the floor. She then sat me down there to see if I would walk for her. She was right. As soon as she sat me down I walked as fast as I could right over to dad and crawled up into his lap. That made mum make a happy sound and it surprised the vet too. She was taken aback by the way that I walked. She wanted to see me walk again so she took me from dad. I clawed, kicked and meowed at her for taking me away from Dad. She set me down and I walked right back to him.

They sat on the floor with me and talked for a while. Mum got me from dad and gave me luvins, then put me back in my carrier. I was thinking that this was not a bad trip to the vet at all and maybe they were done already. I was wrong. The vet told mum she was going to take me back for some tests and to be examined by more people. It was a learning place and I was so different that they wanted the other students to get a chance to meet me. That made me feel special and I wouldn't mind meeting the other people; especially if they were all as nice as this vet. I would, however, very much rather rather meet them with mum and dad with me. She picked me up and off I went. I meowed at mum and dad on my way out for good measure.

I was back there for a long time; Mum said it was several hours. There were a lot of different people who came to visit me and every single one of them was really nice. There was one person there who was in charge. He was the teacher for all of the other student vets. He was really good and gentle with me and spent a long time asking his students questions about what they thought was wrong with me, what tests they thought should be done and a lot of other stuff that I didn't really understand.

I just kept telling myself that I was going to be able to go home. I knew mum and dad were both waiting for me and that they were close. Every now and then I would give a really loud meow to try to let them know I was okay.

They finally put me back in my carrier and I knew that meant I was about to go see mum and dad. The nice lady vet then took me back into the same room I was in before. I was so happy to see mum and dad were there waiting for me. Mum got me out of my carrier and gave me some luvins while they talked to the vet. Before I knew it mum was crying.

The vet told mum that everyone there had just fallen in love with me. She said I had been really good and even purred for them. She said that she wished it wasn't so but that she had bad news concerning my diagnosis. They determined that I had Myasthenia Gravis. What that meant was that my nerves couldn't tell my muscles what to do and that without treatment it would get worse. Eventually I wouldn't be able to swallow and I would die. They said that there was a treatment that could significantly slow the progression and allow me to live a life that is my normal. The only problem is the treatment would kill me if the diagnosis was wrong. On top of that the test that would confirm the diagnosis was over two thousand dollars.

Poor mum was so upset. The tears were just falling from her eyes onto the floor. Dad put his arm around her and hugged her. She said she didn't know what to do. They didn't have that kind of money to be able to get me the tests, but she couldn't bear to watch me suffer and die. The vet said that I was fine right now but that without treatment, at some point, they would have to make the decision to send me to the rainbow bridge because I would be suffering too much.

Dad took a deep breath and wiped away his own tears. He said that they would figure it out. We couldn't schedule the tests that day but he and mum would go home and find some way to make it happen. He told the vet about my wonderful Facebook friends from my page. He told mum that he knew they had never asked anyone for that kind of help before but that I was worth setting their pride aside and asking for the help I needed. He had faith that my Facebook family would come through for me. Mum was so sad she could barely talk but she nodded her head. The vet's eyes had watered up as well and she said they would be out in a few minutes with our paperwork and we could leave.

As it turned out that wonderful vet paid our bill for us that day. Mum was speechless. Dad had to wipe away another tear. The receptionists said nice things to me and even had a treat for me as we left.

Mum held me tight the entire drive. They talked some serious adult talk and seemed to make up their minds about what to do before we got home. Neither of them was happy about asking for help but they had already spent hundreds of dollars over the last couple of weeks at the other vets.

Mum said that the Facebook cat community is full of very big hearted people who are always seeing pages asking for help. It can be overwhelming and emotionally draining for them at times and mum really didn't want my page to contribute to that. She also knew there were people out there who took advantage of that community's big heart and there were also people running scams. Mum had always been one who gave to others in need and now she knew what it felt like to be the one in need. She was going to make sure everyone knew what it was that I needed. She would show them the list the vet had given her listing each test and all of the costs. She wanted to be sure that my friends knew that we wouldn't take one dime more than was necessary.

Chapter Eight – FEATHER DAN

Neuro Dan - Feather Dan
March 28, 2015 ·

Today I decided I was bored with the view from my special ledge (the lowest) on the cat tree. I ventured to the couch twice to see what I could see. This made mum extra happy because she could watch TV with me. It's the little things in life that makes us happy. - love Neuro Dan.

Over the next few days mum helped me talk to my friends on Facebook through my posts. She posted a copy of the estimates that the vet had given her and explained everything that was going on. We were all surprised at how many people started to send donations. It was amazing and humbling. Mum even said that her faith in humanity had been restored.

I was having fun playing on my ledge. With all of the toys dad kept changing up and hanging in different places, it was hard to be bored. Even Leroy got hooked on playing with all of the fun. Mum and dad would go buy me new toys all the time. I kept trying to tell them to stick with those feathers toys because they were my favorite.

One day they went to a Renaissance Festival and when they came back they had a bag full of giant colorful feathers. Dad said they were called a peacock feather. He played with me, flipping that big feather all over my ledge and around the cat tree. He snuck it under me and it would pop up from below. I got so excited that I started honking like a goose. Mum got to laughing so hard that she had to sit down. Dad flipped the feather around and let me sniff the stem. I gave it a couple of sniffs, and then gave it one giant savage chomp. The feather made this fantastic crunching noise and I got really excited. I chomped it again, and again. I chomped that feather over and over working my way back and forth on it trying to find the best places to get that crunch sound.

Mum and dad were laughing at the faces I was making. My nose would get crunched up and dad said I looked like a savage lion. Mum said I had just earned another name and that's when she said I was also going to be called Feather Dan. So that's the rest of the story on how I got my name Neuro Dan – Feather Dan.

I know I had just planned on telling you about how I got my unique name and now you know but I think it would be rude to stop telling my story right now. I included so much other parts of the story that I think I should just keep going. I wouldn't want to leave you wondering about everything that had been going on.

Plus, I'm just about to surprise mum and there are still a lot of other stories that I love telling. So I will continue.

I'd been having so much fun that the next night when mum and dad were having couch time I decided that I wanted to have some couch time too. Listening to them was fun and I had a great view from my perch, but the couple of times mum had taken me up to the couch with her were pretty nice too.

I eased myself off my ledge and started crawling my way over to mum. She and dad were watching TV so mum got all surprised when she saw me walking across the living room. She nudged dad and told him to take a look. She probably thought I was on a floor adventure but I had a surprise for her. I kept on walking towards her. I had to stop once and rest but that was it. I walked right up to the couch next to her feet, got up on my hind legs and tried to hop up. It was just a little too high for me but mum was delighted and she reached down to help me up. I looked around and decided that I needed some rest so I curled up next to her and purred. Mum was so happy. She gave me extra luvins and I took a little nap.

When I woke up I was feeling frisky. Mum had gone to the kitchen to get a drink but dad was still on the couch. Dad didn't see me wake up but he heard me call for him. I had propped myself up so my back legs were on the couch and my front legs were up on a squished couch cushion. Then I chirped at him to get his attention.

I wanted to play. Dad told mum to come look at me and he grabbed my peacock feather. He got that feather to dance and jump all over that cushion. My eyes got wide and I leapt as high up on that cushion as I could in order to try to catch it. Mum laughed out loud and said I looked like I had frog legs from her angle. She was amazed and just stood there and watched me play. She grabbed a couple different toys for me, looked at dad and said she would sit somewhere else on the couch so I could keep playing.

I played on and off for the rest of the night and had the most fun I'd had since I got there. In between my playing, mum would come over and give me luvins and tell me how happy I made her. When they were getting ready to go to bed I had sprawled out on the couch and was relaxing. Dad asked mum if he should take me back to my ledge and mum told him no, that I looked happy and I would go back there if I wanted to.

That was a big moment for me. I spent the next couple of weeks splitting my time between the couch and my ledge. My ledge was about the only place that mum could get me to eat without any issues. It was just perfect for keeping me at the right angle and my head stable. That was where I would eat almost all of my meals all the time no matter where I decided I wanted to hang out.

It took less than two weeks after mum asked my Facebook friends for help before they got all the money that I needed for my return visit to Auburn. A good friend of hers, Patti, who was also a friend of KT and Misfits Critter Farm, had been following me since KT first mentioned me on Misfits Facebook page. Patti said she was considering adopting me before KT found me a home. She decided she was going to pay for half of my tests because I had won her heart. KT was helping to share my Facebook page and I kept getting more and more friends. They were all so nice and I had such a good time listening to mum read their comments to me. A lot of new friends even donated to help me get my tests.

Everyone's generosity made mum so happy that she cried. She was so afraid she wasn't going to be able to help me and she couldn't imagine watching me suffer like that. She called Auburn and got my follow-up visit scheduled. They got it scheduled for the very next week which mum said was really fast for a place like that.

My appointment was on a Tuesday so both mum and dad had to take the day off but, neither of them seemed to mind. Just like the first time, we got up really early. I don't usually eat that well if it's too early. That's when I get my lunch dates with gramma but this time I knew mum was already pretty nervous about this visit so I ate well for her.

After breakfast we were out the door, in the car and on our way to Auburn. That three hour drive sure did feel like it took a long time. I tried to nap on mums lap but I just can't relax on a car ride. Mum made sure to let dad know when his driving made my claws dig into her legs. Poor dad was trying but he said bad drivers were making him have to hit the brakes too often.

By the time we got there, we were all ready to be out of the car. The receptionists were really nice to me again. Once we were signed in, we walked down the long hall to the same waiting room we were in the last time. There was a couple more people there than the last time but everyone was quiet and their animals were all well behaved. The vet came out and told us which room we would be going to and just like last time, we got back pretty quick.

The vet didn't make me do any walking or anything this time. She just gave me a quick look over and told mum and dad they needed to get started. She said there were a lot of tests and it was going to be several hours. She told them to go find lunch, gave them some recommendations and let them know she would call when I was ready. Mum and dad gave me some quick luvins and there I went back into rooms with the poking and prodding things.

I don't even want to talk about all the tests that they did that day. I know they were necessary but some of them really didn't feel good. I was brave though and I let the vets do what they needed to. I didn't even try to bite anyone. It felt like it took hours and mum later told me that it did. I was extremely relieved but also in a really grumpy mood by the time it was over with.

The vet talked with mum and dad in the exam room. They told them just how brave I had been and even let them know that I purred for them when they stopped poking me and started petting me. They talked about my diagnosis and what the results would mean.

There are two different types of Myasthenia Gravis, acquired and congenital. They said that acquired usually happened due to an infectious process and that it can be reversed with medication by getting rid of the infection. Unfortunately, there is no medication or reversal of the congenital type. They showed mum and dad some physical therapy techniques that they said could help build some strength and gain more flexibility in my front legs. They said it would take a couple of days before the test results were going to come in so we were able to go.

Mum went to the desk and paid for the tests and off we went. The ride back was just like the last time. Mum and dad talked about what they should do depending on the diagnosis. They decided that if it was congenital and nothing could be done that they would give me the best life they could for as long as possible. Dad said I was a stubborn fighter and that I didn't know how to quit. He said that as long as I was going to fight, he'd do whatever it took and fight with me. He looked at me and told me "You fight and I'll fight."

I was pretty exhausted when we got home, so I spent most of the day relaxing on my ledge. Leroy came to check on me a few times. I think he could tell I'd had a bad day because he was being extra nice to me. Grace didn't bother me at all, she just curled up in her spot in the living room or followed dad around. Even Amelia seemed like she felt bad for me because she curled up in the tube part of the cat tree above me and took a nap when I did. That was about the closest thing to snuggle that she has ever done.

It took a few days before the test results came back in. During that time I got another visit from gramma and gramma-great. I loved it when they stopped in to see me. I also wound up with a sink bath, got mad and bit dad on the pinky. I was also starting to spend more of my time on the couch. I decided that when

mum and dad had their eight o'clock couch time, I
wanted to be there too. Mum gave up her normal spot
on the couch next to dad and moved over to sit in
front of him instead so I could have the spot where I
liked to play. Dad was getting really good at playing
with the feathers and I was having the time of my life.

When mum got the phone call from Auburn she
was only on the phone for a minute and when she
hung up she started to cry. My disease was congenital
and there was nothing anyone could do. She curled up
on the couch with me and snuggled until her eyes
stopped leaking. I tried to let her know that I was
happy and not scared at all. She then got out her
laptop and started typing on my Facebook page to
update my friends. This is what I watched her write:

Neuro Dan - Feather Dan

April 14, 2015 ·

*Neuro Dan's mum here. I got the call I have been
waiting for from the Vet today. It isn't good. His
myasthenia gravis is congenital, which means there is
no way to help him get better. All we can do is treat
symptoms as they arise. I am heartbroken. I love this
little man so much. He deserves the world and I will
continue trying to give it to him. He is happy and
loves life right now. I will do everything in my power
to make sure he remains the precious, happy-go-lucky
soul he is. Thank you for all your prayers and
thoughts. We could not have done it without you. Just
keep them coming so he can live a beautiful life
without progression of the disease.*

She got a lot of people who responded to her. They
all were so kind and gave her words of

67

encouragement. They gave her names of people to talk to that might have some ideas. She listened to everyone and seemed to get into a little bit of a better mood.

When dad got home from work she told him what the diagnosis was. He looked sad for a minute and came over to sit with me. I wasn't feeling sad though, I was feeling rather frisky. I chirped at him and pounced on a cushion to let him know I wanted to play. Dad shrugged his shoulders and told mum that I sure didn't look like I was upset or progressing. He told her I was a fighter and he bet that it would be a long time before that disease would progress enough to slow me down. Mum told him he was right, so they both played with me and instead of having the sads we all had a fun night.

Chapter Nine – I got mail!

Neuro Dan - Feather Dan
April 23, 2015 ·

*Today was a huge day for me. I finally figured out
how to get down off the cat tree shelf without hurting
myself. All I have to do is back up! I got down and
played with my toy THREE TIMES TODAY! Mum is
so happy* 🖤🖤🖤

I had been making it a habit to be on the couch
with mum and dad by the time they sat down in the
evenings. I would get down from my ledge after my
dinner each day, but I was getting tired of falling on
my face every time I jumped down. It finally dawned

on me that I could just turn around and back up off the ledge. I tried it and even though it was weird not being able to see where I was going it was much better than jumping down and banging my chin on the ground. Mum saw me back off and she got really excited for me. She got so excited that she called dad at work to tell him about it. Mum gets really excited about the little things.

I went over to a new toy that sat on the ground by the cat tree. It was a round disc with a white ball that I could swat and it would zoom around a track in circles. It also had a middle that was really good for sharpening claws on. Leroy tried to do it and he wound up picking up the entire toy. He then decided he would stick to using heavier and bigger things like the cat tree and scratching posts. Amelia tried it a couple of times but she didn't seem too interested in it. She was always more interested in the pile of toys that were up on the very top of the cat tree.

I played with that toy for a while, and then relaxed next to it until mum fed me my breakfast. She left me on my ledge when she went to work but I got down by myself again and kept on playing until it was nap time. That evening, I even got back down again after dinner. I was having fun showing off how good I was getting off my ledge and my chin thanked me for not falling on it again.

That night while I was on the couch playing with my feathers, mum was telling dad about something crazy that happened at work. She had to go to court to testify on a case for her job and she said that the lawyer asked her about me. Why in the world would a judge and a lawyer be interested in me? Mum was so surprised by it that she shared that with my Facebook friends and they came to the conclusion that I must be getting famous. I don't know about being famous but I hope mum said nice things about me to the judge.

Sunday came around and I got to spend the day with dad again. We had lots of time to snuggle and I was feeling extra playful so he played with me a lot. He even told mum that I was going nonstop and he couldn't believe how much energy and stamina I was building up. Sunday was my favorite day of the week because of all the extra play time I got. Mum was so impressed she even shared with my Facebook friends. She had been telling everyone about how my day was going every single day and even putting a picture of me up too. My plan to get JuJu a way to check on me was a huge success. It worked better than I ever thought it would and that made me happy.

The next week I started getting mail from my friends on Facebook. Mum sure was surprised and so was I. I got a package that was full of different kinds of treats, toys and a very sweet card from the sender that told me how much they loved me and wanted me to have fun and be happy. Mum told me that I was very special and that not many kitties got mail of their own. I decided that I would have to share my treats with Leroy and Amelia because I didn't want to be selfish. They both got really excited and I started getting treats every night during couch time.

It wouldn't take long and the mail man even knew me by name. He asked dad once who I was because my name was different. When dad told him about me and my Facebook page, he had a bewildered look on his face and asked dad if his cat was really getting mail. Dad told him yes. Over the years when mum and dad checked the mail, if the mailman was there, they would ask if I had packages. He would always shake his head in disbelief and hand over several packages at a time.

The next night during my play time, mum told me about another Facebook page. They were called Gilberts Auction Page. She told me that they got donations of different items from their fans and then they listed them on their site for people to bid on. Gilbert's mum would take all of the money from the auctions and help other kitties in need. Mum told me that this month I was one of the kitties that they had decided to help out with. Wow! I was really flattered; embarrassed almost. I couldn't believe people cared so much about me. It hadn't been long ago that I was in a rescue hiding from other cats and looking forward to the time I got to spend with KT. It dawned on me just how wonderful my life had become. I hoped JuJu was watching. I played with extra zest that night.

The next night I was on the couch getting my play time and I heard mum talking about my birthday. She was telling dad that I would be one year old in about two weeks. She even told all my friends on Facebook about it. She was trying to think of some fun ideas that she could do for a birthday party for me.

I was surprised to hear this because I didn't think kitties got birthday parties. KT sure did know what she was doing when she sent me here. It seemed like every night there was a new fun surprise and once again I hoped JuJu was seeing this. She'd be absolutely rolling on her back laughing at the idea of little me getting a big birthday party.

My friends had lots of different ideas and I thought they all sounded great. They told mum to bake me a tuna cake and have lots of catnip. That would be great; I'd never had tuna cake I hoped mum was paying attention. Someone else said fill the house with empty boxes because that would be like a bounce house for cats.

I don't think my friends ever knew about Leroy's box obsession. Anytime there was an empty box in the house he had to go in it. It didn't matter what size the box was either. Somehow, he'd find a way to at least squeeze his head inside. Once his head was inside I'm pretty sure he thought all of him was inside and that he was invisible. He was always lots of entertainment when there were empty boxes around.

Someone else had the idea to ask friends for donations and then send all the money to a charity. That got my attention right away. I thought that was a truly wonderful idea. Hundreds of my friends had rallied to me and supported me when I needed it. I could think of nothing better to do than to donate my birthday to a charity. Mum and I were going to have a long conversation about this one. I was even going to use my special "please eyes" on her for it. She said we had time to think it over but it sounded like a great idea to her too.

Later that week dad told me that the coming Sunday was a special day. He said it was a day called Mother's Day and he thought we should do something special for mum. I thought that would be lots of fun and I'd like to do something special for mum but I didn't know what to do. Dad said he would make sure there were flowers and chocolates for her when she woke up in the morning and that he would help me write her a card.

When Sunday came around dad snuck into the back bedroom where he had hidden the flowers the day before. He got them set up on mum's desk with the card and chocolates before she got out of bed. When she got up, she went about doing her normal morning routine. She stopped for a minute and scratched me on my head, then went into the kitchen and made some coffee. She was almost all the way to her desk before she saw the flowers. She made a happy squeaky noise, smelled the flowers and read the card.

Dad got a great big hug and then she came and sat down with me. She forgot all about that cup of coffee. She sat with me and gave me luvins for a long time. I didn't know that would make her so happy but it did and she walked around with a big smile on her face for the rest of the day. That night she even let me wish all the moms of fur-babies a happy Mother's Day on my Facebook page. That made a bunch of other mums really happy. I was learning quickly that it really isn't very hard to make other people happy. Sometimes those little things go a long way. I would remember that because I was feeling pretty happy too.

Chapter Ten – BLANKETS MOUNTAIN

Neuro Dan - Feather Dan
May 27, 2015 ·
Bird? Nope I didn't seez any bird mum. These are just my playtime feathers I promise.

Mum was so happy about her special Mother's Day surprises that she forgot to tell me that I was going to have to go back to see the Vet at Auburn again. I was not happy to hear that at all and I even pleaded with my Facebook friends to talk her out of it. I couldn't imagine what else they could possibly want to do with me. I felt like they must have done all the testing they could and I already had my diagnosis so I didn't understand why I had to go back. Mum said it was because they wanted to examine me and see what, if any, progression my disease had made.

I didn't have to go back for another two weeks so I decided not to worry over it. I decided to keep playing with my feathers instead. At that point in time, I decided that I really didn't need to be on my ledge so much anymore. I was having a lot of fun on the couch and it was easier for me to get down from when I wanted to go on a floor adventure.

Dad had stacked up blankets on the floor at one end of the couch so I could walk up the blankets and even climb my way back up on the couch without too much trouble. Speaking of trouble, I may have started to do my business on the couch in the middle of the night. During the day time I would usually go to the floor but at night I just went to a spot on the couch I wasn't using and went there. Dad was not very amused by that and mum tried hard to help figure out what they could do.

Mum got a special cleaning solution that worked pretty well but it wasn't quite good enough. It wasn't intentional but after a couple of weeks I had covered quite a bit of the couch in messes. Mum started putting blankets all over the couch and while that caught my surprises it didn't stop things from soaking through. Mum was nice and decided we wouldn't share this part of my story with my friends on Facebook. She decided it would just be one of those things we would have to struggle with until we got it figured out.

Mum got a lot of blankets. Dad took the blankets and wrapped up every cushion really good. They'd swap out the blankets for new blankets and wash the dirty ones a couple of times a week. Mum had to get more and more blankets. She got some cheap blankets and some expensive blankets trying to see which ones they thought would work the best.

The pile of blankets got pretty big and mum couldn't figure out where to store them all so she wound up stacking them up at the end of the couch closest to where the cat tree was. The pile would grow and shrink throughout the week as they used and washed blankets. Mum and dad both got in the habit of looking for and getting new blankets when they found good ones.

That stack of blankets eventually got so big that dad called it my Blankets Mountain. Once I got up on that stack of blankets the very first time, I decided it was my favorite spot in the house. It had a view of just about everything. It let me get up higher than anywhere else in the house that I was able to get to. Dad stacked up blankets next to the blankets so it was a double stack and worked like a ramp allowing me to walk right up to the top.

Blankets Mountain put me right in the middle of all the action too. Every time anyone walked down the hall, to the kitchen, or into the living room, they walked right past me. Mum said it was impossible to walk past me without giving me a little luvins or at

least a quick scratch on the head. Dad got good at
playing with me there too. He would hide feathers
and toys all over the mountain and in between
blankets and cushions. I would spend hours hunting
down those hidden feathers and would leave a pile of
loot to show off to him when he came home.

Once I started staying on Blankets Mountain I
decided on one spot on the couch that I would always
do my business on. Gramma was over one day for a
lunch date and she had a great idea that she shared
with mum. She told mum we should just take some of
the dog wee wee pads and put them under the
blankets. That way it wouldn't soak through to the
couch and we could just change the pads. Dad said
gramma was a genius and wished he had thought of
that a long time ago.

When dad got home he pulled all the blankets off
the couch and covered the entire thing with pads.
Then he put the blankets back on. He picked me up
and set me down but I didn't have to go. I did sniff
around because I had been watching him and was
making sure none of my feathers got caught up and
buried where I couldn't get it. All of my feathers were
safe so I climbed back up to my spot on Blankets
Mountain and played for a while.

After dinner that night I did my business and
gramma's plan was a huge success. Dad was thrilled
and laughed with mum. He told her he never thought
that he would be so happy about anything that had to
do with a cat's business. Mum agreed and said I was
worth every bit of the struggle and that this was
probably going to be the permanent solution to that
particular problem. She was right. I took care of

things there almost all the time. Now and then I'd get caught on a floor adventure and I'd have to leave a surprise for dad to find in the morning but not very often.

I also got fewer sink baths because my claws didn't get caught as bad and it was much easier for me to navigate. Mum and dad learned that they would always have to lift a blanket and check the pad under it before they could sit on the couch but it just became habit for them and they never complained to me about it.

When mum and dad weren't home Grace would sometimes hop up on the couch and nap there instead of her spot on the floor. Mum would fuss if she saw her on the couch but I never told on Grace. That way she could enjoy it during the day. She continued to impress me with how nice she was. If I wanted to get off Blankets Mountain and go to another part of the couch all I had to do was get down and nudge her and she would jump right off the couch and out of my way without any complaint.

I got so caught up in the fun of playing on Blankets Mountain that before I knew it mum was putting me in my carrier again. It was time for me to go back to Auburn. It was just like last time. Mum let me sit in her lap and look out the window. She also snuggled me during the drive there. Dad drove and mum kept telling him to drive better so she wouldn't get scratched by my claws, and before we knew it, we were there.

The girls at the front desk remembered me and promised me another treat when it was time to go. The waiting room was pretty quiet and we didn't have to wait long at all. They took me back and after about an hour it was done. They didn't do much with me this time. I was especially happy that no needles were involved. They mostly just tried to get me to walk around and move a lot but I don't do that when I'm at the vet. I hunker down and don't move. They wound up picking me up and stretching out my legs and checked me out pretty good, and then back to the exam room I went.

I was so excited to be back to mum and dad that I wasn't paying attention to what the vet was talking about. Whatever he said it made mum start crying again. I was trying to figure out why and tell mum that I was just fine. Dad gave mum a hug and we were on our way. I got my treat at the front desk and when we got in the car mum started writing something to my Facebook page. I watched her write it and this is what she wrote.

Neuro Dan - Feather Dan

June 1, 2015 ·

It is with sobs and tears that I write this post. Dan does not have MG. he has a progressive motor neuron disease that affects from his ribs up to his cranial nerves. It is congenital and it is progressive. The doctors at Auburn have given him 1.5 to 2 years to live. It is also affecting his vegas nerve which is responsible for digestion and cardio issues. There is no treatment. Aspiration pneumonia is usually the issue that becomes fatal for this disease. I do want to point out that another Facebook cat has symptoms very similar to Dan. The doc said she wouldn't live a year and she is turning 7 this month! Love to all of

Dan's friends. We are going to love him as long as we can and then some!

So those doctors didn't think I had very long left to live. I was about to turn one and they told mum I'd be lucky to make it to two years old. At first that made me sad because I really loved my life, so I cuddled really hard with mum on the drive home. Dad was always optimistic and he told mum that maybe they were right but he just didn't think so. He said I just had too much life in me. He said you could still just take one look into my eyes and see how much I loved my life and he just didn't believe it would happen that fast.

When we got home mum set me on Blankets Mountain. I got one look at my feathers and decided to goose honk at dad. I wanted to play! I knew he was right and I just wasn't going to worry about it. I didn't know what the progression would be like but right now I really just wanted to play. Dad chuckled and told mum "I told you so." He then played with me till I was ready to rest.

Mum had been doing research and talking to other friends. She found out that one of the things that I needed to avoid was being stressed out. Stress was something that could trigger my disease to progress. She discovered that the progression could happen in many ways. It could start and move quickly, be slow over time, start then stop and start again later. I didn't have any stress at all at home so that made me feel pretty good.

Chapter Eleven – my absolute most number one don't like of the trip to the vets

Neuro Dan - Feather Dan

June 11, 2015 ·

Guess who came to visit me today! Mum got to tag along with gramma and brought more mats and treats! I was scared at first but when I figured out who it was I went bonkers. Mum said she had never seen me give mushes and head bonks that hard. They stayed for a few hours while I settled in for a nap on my mum. I was sad when she had to go but she said she is coming back day after tomorrow!!! I'm hanging in there. Just ready to come home.

A few days later, mum came to tell me good morning and give me luvins. She told me that it was my birthday and that meant that I was going to get all kinds of presents and treats. Some of my Facebook friends sent me birthday cards and even some packages. We sat down that night and opened all of my presents and cards. I got lots of different types of treats and some were even from Europe. Wow! I couldn't believe that people sent me treats from all the way across an ocean.

I had so many treats that night I almost couldn't play with my feathers but some of my other presents were brand new feather toys. I couldn't pass up on playing with new feather toys. I even got some real feathers and I just have to give every feather lots of chomps until I don't hear that crunchy noise anymore. When the crunchy noise stopped, that's when it was time to have dad make them jump around on top of the cushions, so I could jump up and pounce them.

Mum opened all of the cards and read each one to me. I had a bunch of them and even some that were homemade. I had some really creative friends that made some beautiful cards for me. People even wrote me notes and stories in the cards. Some of them told me about their kitties, some told me where they were from, some told me about how much they were inspired by me but all of them told me how much they loved me.

The next day mum told me I had an appointment with a different vet. She was going to look into some other forms of treatments that some Facebook friends had recommended. She said the lady we were going to see did what was called cold laser therapy. Mum tried to explain to me what that meant but I didn't really understand all those big words. She scooped me up and off we went.

Gramma went with her on that trip, so at least I was able to sit in mums lap instead of riding in the carrier. The vet lady was very nice, but it was still another visit to another vet. She did some bloodwork on me and that meant pokes with the needles again. She thought I was dehydrated so I got another poke and some fluids. The vet said I had a bladder infection and that she could take care of that but she was also worried that I was in the beginning stages of renal failure.

I didn't know what that meant but I guess mum did because she was back to crying again. I really hated to see mum crying every time we went to the vet. I knew that meant that there was more bad news and I really thought that, maybe, enough could just be enough. I didn't feel like anything was wrong but poor mum was crying again. Gramma looked pretty worried too but she was like dad and could be pretty optimistic. She told mum not to worry until after the bloodwork results came back. I agreed with gramma and I guess so did mum because she stopped crying and got back to giving me some good luvins.

When I got home I had even more mail waiting for me and more feathers came for me to play with. I forgot all about that vet visit and got right to playing with those new feathers. Gramma made sure we all got treats and she even gave Grace two bones to chew on before she left. I played for a while but I was pretty tired from the vet visit, so I spent most of that night snuggling with mum.

A couple days went by and mum got a phone call that put her in a good mood. As it turned out I was not having any problems with my kidneys after all. Gramma had been right about staying positive. I was happy to see mum so happy, so I made sure she got extra purrs and even gave her and gramma some wet face mushes. Mum always said that my wet face mushes were the best.

I had been getting curious about those chew bones that gramma kept giving to Grace. I wasn't sure why she got so excited about them but I got a notion that I would have to go check them out. I figured I had better do it when Grace was distracted. Sometimes Amelia would try to take them away from Grace while she was chewing on them. Grace would growl at Amelia to tell her no but sometimes Amelia would keep trying. That's when Grace would snarl and push her away with her nose.

I waited for dad to come home. As soon as he got home from work he always set down his work stuff and took Grace out for a walk. I hustled down off Blanket Mountain and shuffled over to one of her bones. She had left one right in the middle of the living room so I didn't have to go very far to get to it. Mum saw me from the kitchen and was watching me but I didn't mind being watched as long as it wasn't by Grace.

I gave it a few good chomps but it didn't make any crunchy noises like my feathers did. Then I hooked it with my paw and tossed it in the air. I batted it around for a minute then pounced on it and kicked it with my back feet a bunch of times. When I heard the door open I gave the bone one last swat before going over to the glass door to look outside.

Grace came back into the living room and sniffed her bone. She looked at me and came over to give me a big sniff, but that was all. She had a pretty good sniffer so I figured she could probably tell I'd been playing with her bone but I didn't try to run off with it like Amelia would, so she didn't seem to mind. She just went back to it and kept on chewing on it. I didn't think that the chew bones made very good toys so Grace didn't have to worry about me borrowing any of her bones.

That night mum got really excited. She said that my Facebook friends did it again. The cold laser therapy that the vet said might help me was really expensive. Mum asked my friends to help if they could and in just two days they did it! It was so humbling when they did it too. I still couldn't believe that so many people loved me so much that they would be so generous. They hadn't even met me but they never hesitated to help me out. I knew I was truly blessed to have such a wonderful family from all over the globe.

The next day I was headed back to the vet again. This was the third different vet that I'd seen. All of the vets were really nice but I really just wanted to be home on Blankets Mountain with my feathers.

This vet visit was different. This one was going to include my absolute most number one doesn't-like of the trip to the vets. I wasn't going to be able to go home with mum. I was going to have to stay there for seven days and six nights. I was so shocked that I didn't even know what to do. Now I understood why dad gave me so many hugs and kisses before he left for work that morning. That was going to be a long, long time. It would be forever before I saw mum again. She was crying again and gramma was trying to help her feel better. Mum promised she would come back and visit me the next day. I knew it was a really long drive; it took us almost two hours to get there. I really wished I could just go with her. I just couldn't imagine being away from home for so long.

When mum got home she told dad she was super worried. She was scared that being away would stress me out and that the stress could trigger my progression. Dad wasn't sure at all about what to do or say with this one except to remember what a fighter I was. Mum kept posting for my Facebook friends for me while I was away.

The treatments weren't painful or anything. I just had to lay there while a machine did something that I couldn't even really feel. I felt better that the treatment didn't hurt and I had a cage all to myself. Mum left me lots of my own blankets and toys, so I snuggled with those and just enjoyed the smell of home. I missed my meal times badly. I loved being able to sit with mum or dad and get my food the right way. Mum had left them with my special food so they did feed it to me. They just didn't sit with me and help. It meant I got a really messy face but they kept cleaning me up.

Just like mum promised she visited me later that day. Both mum and gramma showed up and I was so happy that I sang so loud I almost coughed. Mum sat with me for over two hours and I even fell asleep laying in her lap. She took the time to feed me herself before she left, but I had to spend another night at the vet. Mum said that counted as two days and one night down.

Mum made it back to see me every day. Most of the time gramma was with her. When Saturday came dad was there too. I got so happy that I sang for the entire time they were with me. Dad had asked some questions and had been talking to mum. I really didn't hear much of what they were saying because I was purring so loud but the next thing I knew I was being scooped up and put in my carrier. Dad said I was going home for the rest of the weekend and he would take me back on Monday.

I was so happy when I got home that I meowed over and over again for five whole minutes. Leroy and Grace came up and gave me nose sniffs and big old dog sniffs. Graces tail wagged so hard she knocked a cup off the coffee table. I got right up on top of Blankets Mountain and proceeded to make goose honks at dad. It had been days since I'd been able to play with my feathers and with him. We played for a long time and I took a great big nap right where I had wanted to be all week; surrounded by my family. I was one super happy boy.

That night mum and dad talked. They decided that I wasn't going to spend any more nights at the vet. Even though it was almost a two hour drive, they agreed that they would arrange their schedules and find a way to take me back and forth. The treatments were taking less than thirty minutes and they both agreed that the risk of the stress causing my disease to progress was something they just couldn't take if there was anything that could be done.

For the next week they all took turns taking me. I had to ride in the carrier but at least I got to come home. Some days, dad took me and some days, mum took me. Even gramma took me a couple of times. When gramma took me I got extra treats when I got home and I loved it.

After that second week I only had to go back to get treatments twice a week. That lasted for two more weeks. Then they said that I was done. I wasn't sure if the treatments had helped me or not. I felt the same. Mum and dad could tell I was more playful and energetic than usual but they weren't sure if the treatments were the reason. We never really knew if the cold laser therapy helped, but we did know it didn't hurt me. Mum was always willing to try anything if she thought it would help me be stronger and happier.

Chapter Twelve – Visitors

Neuro Dan - Feather Dan
June 30, 2015 ·

Mum is stuck working late again tonight but I heard dad talking to her on the phone and he said I'd get treats and FEATHERS before she gets home! I'm feeling much better tonight and got to spend time with gramma today (I promised I wouldn't tell how many treats I got). Now if mum would be home it would be a perfect day. - Love you my friends - Neuro Dan

I thought I was off the hook when mum said they decided to stop the cold laser therapy but mum wasn't done trying to help me yet. She had me go back to another vet. This one was nice too and he didn't make mum cry so I liked that. He was the first one who didn't just tell her to enjoy the time she had with me. He said there really wasn't anything that could be done to cure me but there were things we could try to strengthen me and make me feel even better.

They talked about stretches and other ways to strengthen muscles. We'd tried that before and most of those things hurt my shoulder blades. Sometimes, I would get mad about it, so mum didn't push me too much with physical therapy. They also talked about acupuncture. I wasn't so sure how I felt about some lady sticking me all over with needles. Mum told me it wouldn't be like the needles that draw blood and stuff it would be different. She even said it would be relaxing. Well I didn't see her volunteering to get poked with me but I'd trust her anyway.

Of course, that meant more trips to the vet each week. It meant more car rides, more being checked out by strangers, but it also meant I got to get a lot of extra treats and snuggles. I was getting really good at giving everyone "the eyes" and always got treats when I did. When gramma took me, I didn't even have to give her the eyes. She just started giving me lots of treats right away. Sometimes, I could get even more extra treats if I gave her the eyes, which of course I did.

Mum was right. The needles really didn't hurt and the lady who did it would sit with me, talk to me and pet my head to keep me relaxed. She was extra nice and even she gave me extra treats when the treatment was done if I gave her the eyes.

I was going to have to teach Leroy and Amelia how to do "the eyes" look because they didn't seem to understand how well it worked. Grace had her own version of "the eyes," but she used her nose instead. She gave what dad called nose pokes. She'd poke him in the leg with her nose over and over again until she either got a treat or a bone. Sometimes she even got both!

The trips to the vet became a routine for all of us but lots of other stuff was happening at the same time. I started getting visitors. Some of my Facebook friends liked me so much that they wanted to know if they could visit if they were in the area. Mum and dad talked about that for a while. Dad was always pretty security-conscious and was skeptical about it at first but mum felt pretty good about it. They agreed that I could get visitors and my first ones showed up not long after.

They were two super nice ladies named Catherine and Tina. They were very friendly and I could tell as soon as they looked at me that they loved me very much. Mum told me they had been following my story on Facebook for a long time and I enjoyed being able to meet some of my friends face-to-face. They brought me presents too! I got extra treats and feathers toys. Anytime I get extra treats and new feathers toys, I get excited. They stayed for a while and talked with mum while they took turns giving me luvins, but before I knew it, they had to go. I really enjoyed my visit with them and was so happy mum talked dad into letting me get visitors now and then.

I also kept getting packages and letters in the mail. Dad said the mail man still gave him a funny look every time he stopped and asked if I had mail. I got more treats from all over the world! Mum said I was getting spoiled and that not many kitties got to try treats from other countries like I did. I even got different feathers. One day I got a surprise that made me do my goose honk. Mum came in with a really long tube and told me it had my name on it. When she opened it and reached in she pulled out a huge pile of real peacock feathers. Holy cat! That was a lot of peacock feathers! They were some of my favorite feathers because they were so long that I could chomp on them for a really long time before they stopped making that fun crunchy noise.

Another day a bird decided to hang out on our porch. I was sitting at the glass door watching the outside. I loved watching the birds fly around and the leaves blow. Part of the day, if it wasn't cloudy, I would enjoy lying in the sun puddles too. One day, a bird decided to hang out on the porch, which got me so excited that I started honking at it.

Dad was home and working on his computer. He jumped right up when I let out three great big goose honks in a row. When he looked over at me I was standing up staring at the top of the porch. My whiskers were spread out, pushed forward and quivering. My eyes were as wide open as they could be. I was so excited that I honked again and made a move like I wanted to pounce up towards the sky. That's when dad saw the bird.

It was flying around and landing on different parts of the porch. It didn't seem like the bird saw either me or dad. It even hung upside down a couple of times. It landed in a plant that was hanging from the ceiling, then dropped down to the porch ledge. It even landed on the ground right in front of me. That was the closest I'd ever been to a bird and I was so excited that I didn't even know what to do, so I started chattering at it.

I guess it still didn't hear me because it hopped right up to me and past me. I bopped my head on the glass trying to get to it and that's when it saw me. It flew back up to the top of porch, looked down at me and squawked at me a couple of times. Then it flew away. Dad must have thought that was pretty funny because he was laughing hard. He had tried to get his camera out to catch me honking, but like always, I stopped honking as soon as I saw he was ready.

Later that month, I got another visitor! Mum was really excited. She said that her name was Patti. She helped me get to Auburn initially. Since then, she and mum had become really good friends. Mum said that it was because of me that they met each other and that I was really special to be able to help her make such a good friend.

When Patti got there, she and mum talked for a long time. She hung out with me on the couch next to Blankets Mountain and gave me lots of luvins and treats. I enjoyed listening to them talk. Their voices were very relaxing to me. I didn't do much playing that day, but Patti had brought me treats and toys anyhow. My collection of toys was getting so big that mum bought me my own kitty toy box to help me keep them organized.

Patti bought me some foam steps to help me get up and down. They were covered in soft fluffy material that was comfortable and felt good to sleep on. They were perfect for getting up and down from the couch and made my life a whole lot easier. Dad would also put them over by the glass door so I could sit up higher and get a better look outside.

I really liked Patti she had a very soothing voice and I was sad to see her go. Mum went with her and they went out to go see dad who was working nearby. Mum came back and realized that they had been having such a good time talking that she forgot to take pictures. I had to remind her that memories are even better than pictures. Mum had to agree with me.

A couple weeks later, there was a holiday that I decided I did not like. Mum said it was the Fourth of July and called Independence Day. She said that it was a national day to celebrate our freedom. I liked the idea of freedom just fine but I did not like the way it was celebrated.

There was a country club really close to where we lived and our glass door faced its direction. They set off fireworks and it was super loud. There was also a house right behind us and those neighbors set off fireworks for hours and hours after the initial fireworks show. The bangs scared all of us. Poor Grace barked at each one and whined and cried for hours. Leroy and Amelia ran off and hid. All I could do was hunker down.

Mum curled up with me on Blankets Mountain and built a little blanket fort around me. She talked to me and gave me luvins all night but I was quivering before the night was over. Dad tried to turn the television up so it would help drown out the noise but it didn't really help. Mum told me it would be over soon and while it didn't feel like soon to me, it did eventually stop. I knew that Leroy and Amelia didn't like it because neither of them came back out that night and it wasn't very often they didn't do that odd patrol thing they always did overnight.

Mum had been talking to one of my friends named Christi who wanted to do something to help me out. She was very nice and had been a friend on my page for a while. She had an idea to make Team Neuro Dan t-shirts. She organized the entire thing and mum posted what she was doing on my page. It was a big hit. I couldn't believe that my friends wanted a t-shirt with a picture of me and my name on it! That made me feel very special and my friends were all really excited about it. They liked their shirts and the money they spent helped me with my acupuncture therapy for a while. Mum said my friends were some of the best most awesome people and we were blessed to know them. I had to agree with her. I loved them to the moon and back.

Chapter Thirteen – Outside Cat DJ

Neuro Dan - Feather Dan

August 9, 2015 ·

Hai my friends. Happy Sunday! Today I met mums porch kitty. He comes around every night for food and water. When I saw him I wagged my tail like a doggie and got really frisky. Mum says I have no fear sometimes. I say I just wanna luv everyone. Sweet dreams

Our next door neighbor was a very nice lady who had two cats and one dog. She also had her daughter and her mother, who lived with her. The cats were inside and outside cats. They seemed like they had a pretty good life. They got to go out when they wanted and come back in when they wanted. Whenever she took the dog out for a bathroom break, the cats would usually come running from the nearby bushes. They knew when it was meal time and they were always home for that.

Grace was able to meet them now and then when dad took her out for a walk. The cats were pretty friendly with Grace because they were used to living with a dog and Grace loved all kitties no matter who's they were. Grace wasn't really good with other dogs because she never had very much interaction with them. She didn't know how to behave or what to do so she normally pulled on the leash and try to say hi but then it would turn into growls and snarls with teeth showing. Dad always explained to other dog owners who might be walking by that Grace wasn't used to other dogs and she wouldn't make a good playmate for them. People seemed to understand and appreciated the warning. The neighbor had been there since mum and dad moved in, so after a couple of years, Grace was finally able to be friendly towards the dog and stop pulling so hard on the leash. I suspect it was because she could sense the other dog liked cats too and it was a way for them to bond.

I was at the glass door looking outside one day when the neighbor lady and dad were both walking their dogs. They stood in front of the porch and talked for a bit. As it turned out the neighbor was about to move. The apartment she was in just wasn't big enough for the three humans. They were making due with a two bedroom but they had turned the living room into a bedroom for her mom. Her mom was becoming more ill and was going to need a room of her own. The neighbor said that a nurse was going to have to start coming around to help out.

She was asking if dad had seen DJ, because he hadn't been around in a couple of days and they were moving that weekend. It wasn't unusual for DJ to be missing for a few days. Sometimes, he got his own notions and went on long adventures. We were never sure where exactly he went, but sometimes he'd be gone for a while. He always came back, announcing himself with lots of meows. He would always mush up on the legs of anyone who was outside. DJ would get food and then stick around again for a while before getting another notion and heading back out on another adventure.

Dad agreed to try to keep an eye out for him but DJ didn't come back before they moved. The lady came back every day looking for him. She'd call his name and she even walked around the entire neighborhood calling for him. Dad helped her look but they just couldn't find him. Dad promised to keep looking and told her that he'd put some food and water out for him if he stopped by. She said she'd keep coming back and checking.

She didn't move far away at all. She only moved to the very front of the apartment complex where there were three bedroom's available. She said it was much better for her family but she was missing DJ. After a few more days went by she came back to talk to dad again. She was crying and her eyes were red. She said that her other kitty had been hit by a car on the main road and crossed the Rainbow Bridge. She was really upset and dad tried to comfort her. She said she was scared for DJ. She knew he'd never be able to just be an inside kitty and her new apartment was right next to the main road. She was terrified that if she did get DJ, the same thing would happen to him that happened to his brother.

She was in tears and she asked dad if he could take care of DJ. She said she would come back with food and try to help as best she could. She missed him, but loved him even more and was willing to let him live somewhere else if it would keep him safe. Dad told her he would do the best he could. He told her he would make sure he had food and water and would even try to get him to the vet if he needed it. He told her he'd try to get him to come inside, but he wasn't sure he would because of me, my brother and sister. She thanked him, gave him a hug and had tears in her eyes when she walked away.

DJ finally did come back a few days later. He was just fine and in very good spirits. He pranced up to dad while he was walking Grace, mushed him on his legs and mushed Grace on her ribs and face. Dad finished up with Grace and came back out onto the porch with some food for DJ.

Later that day, I saw DJ go over to his old porch. The neighbor used to keep lots of plants and decorations out there but those were all gone now. It was obvious DJ was confused. Dad called to him and he came over and mushed on his legs again. When dad showed him the food and water he'd put out, DJ didn't waste any time at all; he dug right in.

I watched everything from my steps by the glass door. Leroy and Grace were both at the door watching too. That must have gotten Amelia's attention because she pranced right over to see what was going on. Of course as Amelia does towards anything that's different, she proceeded to hiss at DJ. Grace didn't like that so she lowered her head and rolled her on her back. Amelia gave one more hiss and stomped over to the cat tree to sulk for a while. Dad tried to get the door open and everyone out of the way, but Grace and Leroy really wanted to try sniff and greet DJ. While DJ was fine with Grace, he wasn't so sure about Leroy. DJ galloped back over to the other porch and perched up on the rail.

Dad shewed Grace and Leroy back inside and called mum on the phone. He let her know that DJ was back and that he already set out food and water for him. He explained the challenge he had with trying to see if DJ would come inside and told her he was going to wait until she got home so they could work as a team. Mum said they could try to put the other animals in the bedroom coax him in with some wet food.

They tried that night but even with everyone but me shut in the bedroom, DJ wasn't interested in coming inside. Mum even tried moving his food bowl just inside the glass doors a couple of feet, but DJ just sat at the threshold and look stubbornly at mum and dad. Mum sat outside with him and he would even hop up in her lap for luvins, but he just didn't want to come inside.

The next day was when DJ figured out that his family had moved. He stuck around on the neighbor's porch and just waited and waited. In the afternoon, cleaners came to make sure the apartment would be ready for a new tenant. DJ heard the door open and ran over to it. He stopped halfway there when he saw people he didn't know carrying buckets in.

They left the door open while they were in there and DJ, being a brave explorer already, decided to go check things out. He walked in and looked around. There was nothing left in there that he could recognize. The ladies in there fussed at him and he ran out. He hopped back on the porch rail and stared inside through the glass door until they were done. He stayed there until dad came out later with Grace and he followed them for their entire walk. He was chattering away at both dad and Grace. I bet he was asking what had happened and where his family had gone.

Dad knew that his mom would come checking on him within another couple of days and he was right. She was so happy to see that DJ was okay that she started crying again. She left dad with some food for him and some of his favorite treats. As it turned out DJ liked Temptations treats just like me! I decided it was my job to make sure that mum got DJ treats a lot so he would know he was loved and welcome here.

Mum and dad decided that they were going to have to get DJ to start hanging out on their porch because they doubted any new neighbors would want someone else's cat on their porch. They made DJ a bed out of some of my blankets and put a good soft one on top so he would have a comfortable place to sleep. They put it right next to the door so he could see inside. They hoped he would get the idea that he could come in. They would let him be an inside outside kitty if he wanted, but mum said Leroy and Amelia were going to have to stay as inside-kitties only just like me.

It didn't take long for DJ to start sleeping on our porch. He seemed pretty comfortable and was always perched in front of the glass door staring inside with his big green eyes. He'd sit there politely and talk to us through the glass when he was ready for his breakfast or dinner. Mum and dad would both spend time outside sitting with him, petting him and giving him luvins. They were hoping that would get him used to the smells of our house and all of us. It did seem to make him more comfortable but, his heart belonged outside in nature and that is where he preferred to stay. DJ simply decided that he was going to be an outside kitty and that was that.

Chapter Fourteen – Giving Back

<u>Neuro Dan - Feather Dan</u>
August 20, 2015 ·
Hai friends. Iz feeling good today! I saw some
FEATHERS flying on the porch today. Mum gave me
belly rubs so I sang her a beautiful song and she
loved it. She took this pic right before I started
singing. Who is ready for Friday? Mum says humans
like Fridays. I loves you all. Sleep with the
angels 🖤<

Mum surprised me and I got another visitor to the
house. His name was Rick and he was very friendly.
Mum said it was obvious that he was a cat person for

two reasons. The first reason was because he had a Facebook page like mine for his own kitties. The second reason was because Grace liked him. Grace was much better with female people than he was with men. She usually got her hackles up and did a lot of growling when we had guy visitors that weren't dad. With Rick, she was just fine. Leroy and Amelia both came out to check him out too. He brought treats with him and we all got to enjoy Temptations. He told me he read my posts every night so he knew how much I liked those. Boy was he right!

He brought me some presents too. One of them was a long stick with a pheasant feather on the end of it. He wiggled that feather all over the place until my whiskers looked like they belonged on a walrus. He played with me for a really long time. He laughed and said he liked the way I jumped up on the cushions after the feathers. He agreed with mum that I looked like a frog from the back when I did my super jumps. Once I got tired and laid down, he gave me gentle luvins. Then Grace decided she wanted to have head scratches so he pets her while he chatted with mum. He stayed for a few hours before he left and mum told him she could tell I'd had a good time. She was right!

A few days later I got more mail. Mum opened it up and told me I just got the sweetest gift ever. She read me the card and it turned out there was a little boy named Damin with special needs who was a friend on my page. Mum said that he had autism. She told me his mum would read him my posts and show him my pictures every night. His mum said that her sweet little boy just absolutely loved me. He told his mum that if I could do it, then so could he. He made

106

me a card himself and that's what mum said was my sweetest gift ever. She said that that special card from that special boy was inspiring to her and made her very happy.

When dad got home from work, mum was excited to show him the card. He thought it was pretty amazing too and came over to the couch to sit down and give me some luvins for a minute. When he sat down he made a funny face and said words mum said I was supposed to cover my ears if I heard. Mum looked over at him and asked what was wrong. Dad stood up, looked behind him and said he forgot to look before he sat down. He sat on one of my surprises and said he just made a poop pancake. Mum got a huge belly laugh out of that. Dad quickly went off to change clothes and get a shower. When he came back out mum already had the blankets on the couch changed out and he returned to give me luvins. Neither of them ever gave me a hard time about those surprises which I was so grateful for.

One of my friends from my Facebook page had one of his kitties become sick. He already helped me when mum was trying to get me to Auburn. I thought that being willing to help me even when he might not have enough to help his own kitties made him a very special person. He'd been one of my very first friends on my page and knew who I was all the way back from Misfits.

I told mum I wanted to be able to help him back. After discussing it with dad, mum decided that it was okay for me to use my page to help other people. That made me really happy and excited to get to work at helping him. She let me share his story that night and as it turned out a lot of my other friends knew him. Everyone came together to help him get what he needed to help his kitty. Being able to help him made me feel great. I loved being able to use my page to help other people like that and he was incredibly grateful.

There were several times during that time period that I was able to help other people. I was really enjoying it too, but mum said I had to slow down. My friends were so big hearted that she was worried they would give too much too often and it could be bad for them. She said we could still help people but we had to be careful not to overdo it. I sort of understood what she meant but I just wanted to be able to help everyone the way everyone had helped me. I knew mum was right though so I made sure to talk it over with her first.

Mum noticed that for the past week that I had been rubbing at my ears. She looked inside them and even used some Q-tips to try to clean them out. Digging those Q-tips in my ears itched really bad and made me rub my ears for a long time afterwards. She came home one day with something she said was going to help my ears not bother me. She sat down with me and gave me luvins then tilted my head sideways and put drops of something wet in my ears. It certainly wasn't bath level bad but it felt really funny and I didn't like it one bit.

I shook my head and gave her the stink eye. That made her make funny noises and give me lots more luvins. I thought maybe that would be the only time she would do that because I could usually get my way if I gave her the eyes. Giving her the stink eye usually worked well as a way for me to tell her no, but this time it didn't work.

Leroy must have felt bad for me because when I decided to try to sleep it off; he came up and lay down with me. He wasn't much into snuggling so I enjoyed that while I could. I found out that he has ticklish feet because my tail brushed his feet a couple of times which made him twitch and twitch his feet really hard. The next thing I knew, he pulled a leaping Leroy and jumped up and made one giant leap over the couch.

I got those drops in my ears a couple of times a day for a few days. Each time it made me shake my head and I never did like it much, but mum was right and it didn't take very long before my ears stopped being itchy. I wound up getting those drops a few times a year and I never did like it but they always did what mum said they would.

Chapter 15 - Traditions

September 20, 2015 ·
I got to spend all day with Dad and we watched
football all day. Dad gets really excited watching
those games and I got lots of what he called
celebration treats and I really liked that! I hope
everyone had a great weekend. Sleep with the angels
tonight my friends. Love you!

Dad got home early one day and stopped to give
me extra luvins. He told me that mum's birthday was
tomorrow and we were going to make sure she had a
special day. He said that I wasn't allowed to ask
about how old she was going to be. I learned that
people are funny about their birthdays. They enjoy
celebrating them with each other every year but the
older they get the less they want to talk about the
number. Dad told me that we were going to be

celebrating her 29th birthday again. He said they had
been celebrating that one for several years now and
that he wasn't going to break the tradition.

I was also learning that people sure do have a lot
of traditions. I didn't mind because I thought it was a
lot of fun most of the time. I knew there were a few
traditions that I didn't like such as annual visits to the
vets but other than those it was usually lots of fun.
Plus, it seemed like every time there was a birthday or
holiday I got to see gramma and gramma-great so I
thought maybe it would be a good idea to have even
more.

Dad told me that if I was going to give mum a
surprise, I shouldn't say anything about it until it was
time to give it to her. Mum didn't like surprises and if
she thought there was a present or something
somewhere, she would be sneaky and hunt it down to
peak at it before anyone had a chance to give it to her.
I didn't quite understand that because I absolutely
love to get surprises but I listened to dad. He brought
a card home and said he was going to let it be a
surprise from me, Grace, Leroy and Amelia. He
promised me that mum would really like that. He got
it and some other small surprises. He then went about
finding places to hide them. I didn't think mum would
have enough time to find them even if she knew they
were in the house because dad was really good at
hiding feathers on Blankets Mountain for me to find
and sometimes it would take me all day.

The next morning dad had to get up early for
work. While mum was still sleeping he got her
birthday cards and set them on her desk with a
present. He left for work and a couple of hours later,

111

mum came out. She made her coffee, said hi to me on her way to her desk, and then saw what dad had left for her. She went over and carefully opened everything up. She had a pretty big smile on her face at that point. She came over to tell me thank you and gave me lots of luvins. She got out the Temptations and called for Leroy and Amelia to wake up and come to the living room. Of course, Grace was front and center so mum made sure she got a bone first. She then gave everyone else some treats. That was a pretty good start to the morning and I decided I liked birthdays a lot! We rarely got treats before lunch time so it was an extra special day for us too.

Dad even had flowers delivered for mum. She looked like she loved them a lot. That is when I noticed that she had to tell Leroy not to eat them. Apparently he liked to chew on flowers. I didn't quite understand why he would want to do that, but I would let him have one of my feathers if he would leave mums flowers alone. Later that day Gramma and Gramma-Great stopped by and we got lots of luvins and even more treats. They weren't there long before everyone went out for a birthday dinner. When mum and dad came back, mum had leftovers and we got to have some really good fresh fish. Mum said it was salmon which is one of my absolute favorites. I wished it could be mums birthday every day.

That Sunday I learned about football. As it turned out dad loves watching football as much as I love playing with my feathers. During football season he spends almost the entire day at home watching games and doing something mum told me was Fantasy Football on his computer. Dad's usually a pretty quiet, laid back guy every day of the week but during football games, he sure can get loud. I never heard him yell before until he shouted at the T.V. Mum said that he tended to yell at the referees quite a bit and sometimes even the players. I wondered why they never yelled back but mum assured me they couldn't hear him so no one's feelings were getting hurt.

During some games, he would sit on the couch next to me and play feathers while he watched the game. He usually had some pretty good smelling snacks and food on Sunday too! He had one thing that I thought smelled the best but mum said it would be a bad idea for me to have it. She said it was chicken but that they were hot wings and they would hurt my mouth and tongue if I ate them. I never could understand why dad would want to eat anything that made him sweat and drink lots of water, but he sure did like his wings.

One of the best parts about watching football was that when a team he liked scored, he would give me treats. He'd make sure he mixed up the treats too. Sometimes I would get a Temptation and sometimes I would get a special treat from friends all the way from overseas. I always hoped for lots of scores and I had the best time during those Sunday traditions. I looked forward to Sundays and I was super excited when mum told me that football season happened every year. She said she liked it too, but she also said she felt like what was called a "football widow" during the season because dad was always very focused on his fantasy teams. Well, I'll admit, he sure did spend more time at his computer during the week but it always paid off for me on Sundays. Football

113

season became a tradition that I looked forward to every year.

Another tradition that mum and dad had that I think was my absolute favorite was what they called couch time. They always tried their hardest, no matter what was going on to spend time with each other before bedtime.   This also meant time with me too. For at least two hours every night, we all sat together and played. There were very few times that they didn't manage to spend this special time with me, my brother and sisters.

The first time I remember not getting couch time happened after I saw dad bring home something that mum called a suitcase. He set it down in the middle of the living room, opened it up and asked mum if it would work for her. Grace sniffed it first. Then Leroy hopped inside of it and sprawled out. Mum looked in it and said that everything she wanted to bring would fit fine inside that suitcase Dad said the one they already had would be good enough for him.

I wanted to know why mum and dad needed a suitcase. We never needed one of those before; not even when we went on the long trips to Auburn. I wasn't really fond of the idea of going on adventures outside of the house. I was very attached to Blankets Mountain, my ledge and playing with my feathers. I stood up from the top of Blankets Mountain and gave mum an inquisitive look. She got up and came right over to me. She gave me luvins and I purred and gave her wet-face mushes. She told dad she wasn't sure about leaving without one of the two of them there to be with me.

Wait... she just said they were both going to be going away and leaving me alone. Oh no, that just sounded like the worst idea I've heard ever! I made sure I started to purr louder and gave mum an extra hard wet face mush. She looked right at me, so I gave her the eyes. That seemed like it was working. She told dad she didn't want to go. Dad said the plane tickets and hotel room was already booked and that gramma would make sure I was just fine.

Dad gave mum a hug and told her he didn't like the idea of being away either, but it would only be for a few days. I kept giving mum the eyes and dad told her to just imagine how pretty the leaves were going to look up in the mountains in Maine. He reminded her of how good the lobsters would be, the great hiking they would do, and that friends were there they hadn't seen in years.

Mum finally gave in and said they needed the vacation. She scooted Leroy out of the suitcase and disappeared into the bedroom to pack it. Dad walked into the kitchen and made my dinner before taking me to my ledge and helping me eat. I was planning on how I could either get them to stay, or maybe get them to take me along. I wondered how much room mum would leave in her suitcase and if I could manage to sneak in and smuggle myself inside the luggage. I was also trying to decide how many of my feathers I could take with me and which ones would be the best for a plane trip.

When mum finished packing and came back to the living room, she took over feeding me because she said she wanted to spend more time with me before they left. She talked to me and told me gramma would be coming over and taking care of me. She assured me that meant extra treats and she told me to make sure I didn't give gramma a hard time with my meals. She told me I had to eat all my food and not be picky for her. She said that gramma was a little nervous about being responsible for me, so I had to be good and help her out. I listened to her, but I was still giving her the eyes while trying to narrow down my choices of feathers to bring.

Dad told mum to let him know when I was done and finished with my bathroom business. He wanted to get the blankets changed out and get ready for our nightly couch time. He wanted to get started early, so I could get lots of extra play time in before they left. I always liked the idea of extra play time, so that sounded great to me and I ate my food extra fast.

I got up, turned around and faced the couch. That's what I always did when I was done eating. Both mum and dad knew that meant it was time to give whatever food was left on my plate to Leroy and Amelia, and take me to my business spot on the couch. When I was done, dad scooped me up and set me on top of Blankets Mountain. I did some quick grooming to clean up my dinner mess while dad fixed up the couch, and in no time at all, he helped me over to my favorite playing spot where mum used to sit. That night, we had a marvelous episode of feathers time.

Mum and dad spent the rest of the night giving me extra attention and talking about all plans they had for the next few days. It sure did sound like they were going to do an awful lot in a short time. I wondered if people could really relax while staying so busy. I didn't think there was a better way to relax than either lounging on Blankets Mountain or finding a cozy sun puddle to snooze in.

I loved that we got to have extra play time but the night sure did go by fast. Dad brought the suitcases out into the hallway next to the dining room table so they would be able to grab it and go in the morning. Once they went to bed, I watched Grace sniff the bags, but she didn't spend much time worrying about it. Leroy and Amelia both checked it out. I think Leroy may have had the same plan as me because he would paw at the zippers. Of course, as much as he likes getting in boxes he may have just been hoping to play with it.

He had no luck getting it open at all. I knew if he couldn't get it open with his big strong arms, I didn't have a chance. I took a big breath and curled up to sleep. I'd have to put off my plans of being a stowaway until the morning. There was always a chance they'd open them up and add more stuff and I might get another chance.

Mum and dad got up early the next day. Dad fed me while mum got ready. Mum did open up her suitcase again and started adding things to it that came from the bathroom. When I saw how full it was, and I knew, even as small as I was, that I wasn't going to be squeezing into that. Dad's suitcase was more of a bag and he did the same thing as mum, but his bag was just as full. He even had a hard time getting the zipper closed. That was the end of my plans to get smuggled along.

I got extra luvins before they left. I made sure to give both of them lots of wet-faced mushes. Grace started whining and I think that's when she realized

117

they were leaving. She'd jump up at dad and poke him in the leg like she did when she either wanted to go out or get an extra bone. Dad told her she had to stay home and guard the house. He gave her some scratches behind her ears while mum gave Leroy and Amelia kisses. Mum came back to me and picked me up. She gave me a giant hug and lots of kisses. She then set me back on Blankets Mountain and out the door they went.

Things really weren't any different than when they went to work. Grace snoozed in her spot in the middle of the living room and Leroy and Amelia chased sun puddles. When it was about the same time that mum and dad would normally get home, I heard a key in the lock and the door opened. I stood up and did a big back-arching stretch. I looked down the hall and had a small hope that they changed their minds and had come home to me. But that is when I saw gramma come down the hall with a great big smile.

She spent time sitting with me and giving me luvins. She spent time with Leroy and Amelia. She got Grace's leash and took her outside for her business, and when she came back in she went to the kitchen. I heard the lid on one of my cans of food crack open, which got me to jump up excited. She got my food together then came to pick me up and set me on my ledge. I rarely gave gramma a hard time when she fed me and I made sure I ate all of my food for her that time too.

She gave me an air-lift to the couch and cleaned up after I did my business. She went to mums desk and got the treats out of the bottom drawer. Then we all got extra treats and Grace got her bone. After that, she

118

surprised me by sitting down on the couch and turning on the T.V. I gave her an inquisitive look and she asked me if I wanted to play with my feathers. Well of course I wanted to play with my feathers!! I climbed down off Blankets Mountain and crawled all the way across the couch to her. She picked me up and set me on my playing cushion and played with me for over an hour. She stayed for a long time and even took Grace out again before she left. She gave us all kisses and told us she would be back in the morning for breakfast time.

Gramma came back the next morning just like clockwork and stayed for a long time again. This wasn't so bad. I was missing mum and dad something terrible, but I'd never been able to spend this much fun time with gramma. We were having such an incredible, great time. I actually had someone to spend time with more while they were on vacation than I would have on a normal work day. That evening, when she came back to feed me dinner and play feathers, she showed me pictures of mum and dad on her phone. They were in someplace with both big mountains and lots of water.

Gramma said they went to the ocean and then went to the mountains all in one day! She said they were going to be spending the next day hiking. The next day when gramma came back to feed me dinner again, she showed me more pictures. One of the pictures was of some giant looking beast with some crazy decorations growing out of its head. Gramma said that was a moose and mum and dad were lucky enough to see one. She said they got to watch it for quite a while. I'm not sure why that would be fun

119

because the moose didn't even have feathers but I was happy they were having a good time.

When gramma left she said she would see me again in the morning and to be good because mum and dad would be home the next night. That made me very excited. So excited I got a notion and decided to go on a floor adventure that night. I surprised both Leroy and Amelia while they were doing their strange nightly patrols. Leroy couldn't find me, so he looked all over Blankets Mountain and the rest of the couch. I'd hidden myself under dad's desk. I gave him and Amelia both a little scare when they walked next to me and I stood up to greet him. I didn't see anything as interesting as a moose but I did find what mum would call some dust bunnies and one of them got stuck on the tip of my nose and tickled me.

Gramma was confused when she came to feed me and I wasn't on Blankets Mountain. She looked all over and after a few minutes she finally found me. She laughed at me told me that wasn't what she meant when she told me to behave. I got my breakfast and she came back again for my dinner. She didn't stay late and play feathers, so I guessed that meant mum and dad were going to be home in time for our couch time.

I was right and I got some really good luvins from mum right away. Dad grabbed the leash and I noticed Grace's tail was wagging harder than ever. She was jumping up and down and making squeals of joy. Mum told dad to hurry before she had an accident and he did move a lot quicker than normal. When he got back inside he told mum she was hogging me and he wanted to give me luvins too.

I got some fun feathers time that night. Grace stuck next to dads feet all night too. If he went somewhere she was right on his heels. Leroy and Amelia both came up and got more luvins than they normally would have too. Mum and dad sounded like they had great time, but I could tell they were extremely happy to be back home. Mum made sure to update my Facebook page and as it turns out my Facebook friends missed seeing my posts while they were gone.

September 27, 2015 ·

We got home about an hour ago. I dropped my bags and went to see Dan. He sang so loudly I thought he would wake up the neighborhood. Not only did my mother take care of Dan, which is no small feat, but she played with him, picked up all his dirties and fed the porch kitty and Leroy. The house was in perfect shape. She did what I trusted no one to do and she did it with grace. Thank you mom for all that you do. Love - your daughter.

Chapter Sixteen – Routines

Neuro Dan - Feather Dan
October 16, 2015 ·

Hai my friends. Mum got up this morning and couldn't find me. I wasn't in any of my normal sleeping spots, which of course got her frantic. She looked at the blankets at the end of the couch and

found me looking up smiling at her. Iz got all
burrowed into the blankets cause dad forgot to adjust
the air conditioning and Iz got cold. It's always fun to
play hide and seek with mum. She acts so funny when
I do that. Sleep with the angels my friends. Love you
all! - ND

I spent the next day practicing my stink eye. I
figured I'd try to make it look pretty serious in case
they ever decided to pull out those suitcases again. I
could work on telling them absolutely not! I thought
about maybe giving them the cold shoulder for a
couple of days just to make them feel guilty so they
wouldn't want to do that again, but I just couldn't do
it. I loved them too much and I was just so happy they
were back that I had to get caught up on my luvins
and feathers time.

As it turned out it was actually very fortunate that
they got back when they did. Two days after they got
home I started getting sick again. Poor gramma would
have been really upset if I got sick and mum wasn't
home. I also knew that mum would have been in an
absolute panic if that happened and she was that far
away. My neurological problems started flaring up
and giving me more issues. I was having a harder
than normal time holding my head up and was
making an absolute mess of my face when I ate. I also
couldn't really pounce on my feathers. All I really
wanted to do was just lay my head down and rest.

That night mum told my Facebook friends that I
wasn't feeling well and asked for extra prayers. Mum
always got very concerned when the neurological
issues came up. She knew my condition was

124

progressive and a simple flare up could easily be a permanent set back. There was always a chance that when those things happened it wouldn't just be temporary. So far, every time I had one of these flare-ups, I got back to my normal within a few days.

I decided that night I was going to pass on my feathers time and just let mum love on me. Dad got out my Temptations and I ate a few of those with no problem. That made mum feel a little better but I knew she was still worried.

Mum got up early the next morning to check on me. She talked to me in her soft soothing voice that she always used when I wasn't feeling well, which always helped me relax. I really wasn't feeling very well so I just laid there resting my chin on my paws. Mum picked up my head to take a look and noticed that I had some swelling under my chin. She called gramma and let her know she was going to be taking me to the vet. She kept talking to me while she got ready to go. She made a quick Facebook post updating my friends and asking for more prayers. She was hoping it was something simple like an abscessed tooth but she couldn't tell.

Mum got ready much faster than normal. She picked me up and put me in my carrier with some of my favorite blankets and feathers. Once we got to the car she took me out of the carrier and put me in her lap. It was a short drive to the vet in town and she managed to drive and pet me at the same time. Once we got to the vet, she put me back in my carrier and took me in.

Everyone at the vets was always super nice to me. Some of them were even friends with me on

Facebook and they already knew I was on the way. I got taken back and they told mum that they would call her as soon as they got things figured out. Mum thanked them and called gramma. She and dad were both stuck working that day so she wanted to make sure that gramma could come get me if they got me ready to go before either of them got done with work. Of course gramma said yes.

I knew I got the VIP treatment at the vets but that still didn't spare me from all of the things they do. They didn't waste any time. They checked what mum called my vitals, which I really didn't like. I thought for sure there had to be another way to check my temperature. I'd seen both mum and dad sick and they didn't have their temperatures checked the same way. I wondered if there was a cat union or society that I could write a letter of grievance to. Then they started with the poking and prodding.

It didn't take long and they were done. I heard the doctor tell one of the technicians to get me ready to go home. Then he called mum and they talked for a minute but I couldn't really understand what he was talking about. Mum worked for him many years ago and he always used the big doctor words because he knew mum understood what he was saying.

Gramma came to pick me up. When we got home, she helped me out of my carrier and set me on my ledge on the cat tree. Mum didn't want me to eat before I went to the vet, so gramma was going to make sure I had my lunch. I didn't eat that much but that was just because I wasn't feeling well. When I stood up and turned around, she gave the rest of my food to Leroy and Amelia. She then helped me back up to Blankets Mountain. She gave me some Temptations, and of course I ate those. She sat with me for a while and gave me luvins before she went home.

When mum got home, she sat with me for a while, petting me behind the ears. She then got on her phone to update my Facebook friends. She told them the vet said it wasn't an abscess and believed it was a lymph node. I was getting antibiotics and mum was going to be keeping a close eye on me. Mum always felt very blessed that I had such loving friends and she thanked them for all of their prayers and love. She asked my friends to keep them coming, because it really helped us stay positive when things got tough.

Later that night, mum put up a picture of me on my Facebook page and she told me I looked like a chipmunk. I hadn't seen one of those before but she said they were like smaller funny looking squirrels that usually had food stuffed in their cheeks. I skipped feathers time again that night, but did get some extra treats and luvins. I knew that with all of the prayers from so many friends, I'd be feeling better soon.

I felt the same for the next couple of days. The swelling had moved from under my chin to my right lymph node. It got huge and it made it hard to swallow. I wasn't eating as much as I should have been, but mum said it was enough for now. Mum sure did pour on the extra luvins when I wasn't feeling well.

Dad had been giving me my antibiotic liquid and it tasted awful! Mum made dad give me the antibiotics so I would get mad at him and not at her. Sometimes, mum could be just as sneaky as me! The first time dad gave me the antibiotics I didn't give him any trouble at all but that was just because I didn't know how terrible it was going to taste. After the first time, if I saw that dropper, I'd start swatting my tail and turn away from him. I'd even dig my claws into the blankets and shake my head.

He wound up having to sneak up on me and trick me. I only had to get them twice a day but that was too much as far as I was concerned. The only good thing about it was that I got some of my special treats from Europe after I got my medicine. I had a limited supply of those so mum only brought them out on special occasions, or when I wasn't eating enough.

It took a few days before I was feeling well enough to play with my feathers again. By the time Sunday came around I was feeling frisky and it was the perfect day to feel better because it was football Sunday and dad was home. We had a great time even though he kept giving me that nasty medicine. I ate my lunch and dinner with no problems and got a lot of treats which must have meant dad had a good day with his fantasy football stuff.

After a few days, I finally started to feel like my normal self. Pretty soon I was back to my regular routine of playing with feathers, getting luvins and loving life. Dad gave me those nasty antibiotics for an entire week after I got better. I thought that was just unnecessary and I started working on making him feel guilty about it. Mum said he had to do it so the antibiotics could do their job. All of those prayers from my friends must have helped again too. All of the neurological issues that had flared up and bothered me went away and I was back to my normal self which of course included being happy all of the time.

Later that week, mum said that it was a special day. She said that it was her "gotcha day" for dad. She said it was nineteen years ago that day that they got married. She told me it was a wonderful day. She said they got married outside in some beautiful gardens and they always celebrated that day. She even showed me some pictures she kept in a big book she called an album. It sure did look like it was pretty but I noticed there was only one thing missing. I didn't see any feathers anywhere. I couldn't imagine having such a special day and not having any feathers around to play with.

Once I was feeling better and dad quit giving me the nasty antibiotic stuff, things settled back into their normal routines again. Work kept mum and dad busy. I got plenty of gramma visits. I even got some more treats and feathers in the mail. Yup, the mail man still gave dad funny looks every time they saw each other. Grace did her guard the house thing, which included barking at anyone who walked past the back porch or knocked on the door. She also got both Leroy and Amelia with her pit maneuver on several occasions.

Leroy and Amelia kept doing their strange patrols at night. I asked Leroy one night what they were looking for and he told me not to worry about it. He said that we hadn't had the issue in a while. He told me I'd know why if it ever happened again but there was no need for me to worry about it. That just made me more curious than ever, so I started paying more attention to where they patrolled. I even went on floor adventures a few times and did my own patrols but I couldn't figure it out.

I enjoyed those days that were just the ordinary routine days, where nothing exceptional or overly exciting happened. It felt like that was what life was supposed to be about. Just enjoying each day as they came and finding happiness and joy in those things that you may not even remember later. There were a lot of those days and as long as I got my feathers time and treats I always knew I was blessed. Those days may not come with specific memories but what they do give us is an emotional remembrance and a fondness for where we've been. Once in a while, they even grant us an appreciation for where we are now.

Neuro Dan - Feather Dan

November 13, 2015 ·

Hai furiends. What a great day I had! Mum and dad had to work and my other gramma drove down to see us so my other gramma let her in. So I gotz visited by 2 grammas. Can you believe it? Iz so loved! Sleep with the angels my friends. I luvs you!

One night, while I was waiting for dad to come play feathers, Leroy tried to sit on my head. I have no idea why he tried to sit on my head or what he was thinking. I think there are a lot of times that even Leroy doesn't know what he's thinking or what he's doing. He surprised me though, and to make sure he knew I didn't appreciate that I bit him right on the butt. That shocked him because I bit him pretty hard and he jumped straight up in the air about three feet, landed and ran off like a ghost was chasing him. Of course, that got Grace in hot pursuit mode but he was going so fast she didn't catch him that time.

Mum saw what happened and was trying to control her giggles so he wouldn't think she was laughing at him. Leroy was a big guy but he was also a big softy and got his feelings hurt pretty easily. If he got fussed at for getting into something he wasn't supposed to or if he got laughed at for missing a jump and crashing he could pout for days. He'd get in such a sulky mood that mum would have to go find him and give him special luvins and attention before he'd come back out and join the rest of the house again.

There was one day that week that I was feeling off just a little bit. It wasn't anything serious and I didn't even think mum noticed. I was having some balance issues, which isn't at all unusual with my condition. That day I was headed up my kitty steps and almost fell off twice. Mum happened to be home and was at her desk. She saw it and caught me both times so I didn't get hurt, but it sure made mum nervous.

I absolutely love my steps. When they are pushed in front of the glass door, I can climb up, soak up the sun, watch birds and socialize through the glass with DJ, the porch kitty. I was worried mum was going to take them away because she was very protective of me and didn't want me falling. Unlike most cats, because of my condition, I can't land on my feet. When I fall I'm more likely to land on my side and mum was always concerned about me getting injured.

132

When dad got home, she told him what happened and asked him to help keep an eye on me. She said if I kept falling, she was moving the steps back over to the couch unless she was home to watch me. He had the next day off and told her he would keep a watch.

The next day, dad kept a close eye on me. That was great because it got me extra feathers, treats and luvins. I didn't fall one time and I spent lots of time on my steps. I even got up and down a few times just to show off for him. Leroy entertained us both as he had a bad case of the zoomies for most of the day. There were a couple of times that Grace thought he was speeding too fast. She'd do a popcorn bark and go get him with that pit maneuver. Leroy didn't seem to be nearly as bothered by it as Amelia was, and it rarely deterred him from resuming his racing when he had the zoomies.

I thought that mum was being a little too worried about seeing me fall. That night dad forgot to turn off the air-conditioning and it gave me an idea. I was a bit chilly and thought of the perfect hiding spot to get warmed up, so I decided to play hide and seek with her. When she got up the next morning she couldn't find me anywhere. She looked under her desk, looked under dad's desk, looked all around the couch, and checked the cat tree. She looked behind the TV stand and even in the kitchen, but she couldn't find me anywhere. She had been calling my name and was starting to get a little frantic when she looked at a pile of blankets at the end of the couch and found me looking up at her smiling. I'd pulled a couple of blankets off Blankets Mountain and gotten myself all burrowed into the blankets to get warm. Of course I got lots of luvins once she found me.

The next week mum got a message from KT. She found one of my birth siblings and was able to get a picture. His name was Hamish and KT said he got a home with a really nice man and he was spoiled like me. He said that we had very similar personalities but Hamish got lucky and didn't have any known issues like I did. I got to see the picture and I thought we could certainly be twins. It was nice to see a sibling. I didn't remember how many I had and was taken away from them so soon I could barely remember them. It was nice to know at least one of them got to have a good life like me. I hoped the rest of them did too.

About a week later, I saw something that made me do my goose honk, jump up and go as fast as I could to the glass door. I was relaxing on Blankets Mountain when I saw movement on the porch. I kept looking and I saw a squirrel right there in front of the glass door. I honked again, jumped up and backed right down Blankets Mountain. Then I even jumped off the couch. I didn't even care that I landed and did an ugly face plant. I scurried over to the glass door without stopping once and climbed right up my steps.

Dad watched me and was absolutely bewildered because he'd never seen me do anything that crazy before. When he saw the squirrel, he understood what was going on and watched with me. The squirrel scurried all over the place and checked out everything out there. He hopped up on the rails and climbed up to the top, then jumped down and landed right in front of me. He did a couple of frantic looking tail twitches and sat down. That was when Grace saw what was

134

going on. When she barked she made me and dad both jump, and poor squirrel left a dust cloud behind him because he ran away so fast. He ran to the tree line and was up a tree in about two seconds.

Dad fussed at Grace and then came over and to sit down next to me. We both looked outside and watched the squirrel jump between the trees. Dad said that would probably be the last time that he came onto the porch. After dad said that, I gave Grace an ugly stink-eye look. I was so excited; I just knew I'd be dreaming of squirrels for the rest of the week.

I got more mail that week and mum said it was because it was almost Halloween. She said some of my friends were sending me treats. Dad had the mailman shaking his head again when he stopped to get the mail. The mailman gave him a funny look when he handed over a half a dozen packages and dad told him it was treats for me from my friends for Halloween. The mailman looked absolutely bewildered. I guess he didn't know cats like to get treats on Halloween too. Well, he was getting to learn all sorts of things about what cats like just by being my mailman, and I was happy to help him become more educated.

I had a great time on Halloween. I got lots of different kinds of treats and mum said I needed to slow down and pace myself or I was going to get a tummy ache. She said the kids outside trick or treating would be having the same problem tonight and that part of the fun is to have lots of treats later in the week. We got a couple of kids at the door that night but not many. Grace barked at all of them and dad would just hold her by the couch and let mum give the kids some candy. I stayed on Blankets Mountain and I could see all the kids at the front door and they looked like they were having as much fun as I was.

Of course mum was right about it being more fun to save those treats for later in the week. By the time football Sunday came around I still had lots left. Dad gave me even more than normal. Gramma came over and visited and she gave me even more. Mum got home early that day and I got even more from her. I was wondering how many more treats I could handle before I got that tummy ache that mum was always warning me about.

A couple of weeks later, I got a really big surprise. Mum and dad were working so gramma came over for a visit at an odd time. It wasn't time to eat; it was more in the middle of the day. And unless mum or dad was home, she rarely stopped by at that time. She walked right up to me and gave me some luvins for a minute. Then she took Grace outside to do her business. When they came back in she sat down with me. Gramma told me that I was going to have a special, surprise visitor!

A little while later and her phone rang and gramma talked to someone for just a second and told whoever was on the other end that she was on the way. Gramma disappeared outside, then came and came right back a couple of minutes later. She had a lady with her who I hadn't seen before. I'd never gotten a visitor without mum or dad home, so I was pretty curious about whom this could be. Grace ran over to her and gramma gave Grace's head a gentle rub with the new lady beside her. Grace got happy pretty quickly. Gramma brought her over to dad's desk and gave her some treats to give to Grace. She even gave her a bone. Grace was quite content after that and it looked like she found her new best friend. Then, gramma and this new person came over to see me.

Leroy and Amelia both came out of the bedroom to see what was going on. I was standing up on Blankets Mountain checking everything out. Gramma told me that this lady was my dad's mom. I was shocked. It hadn't dawned on me that I might have TWO grammas. Wow! I had to process this for a minute. She was saying hi to me and she was just as nice as gramma. She got a couple of treats and gave everyone a round of treats. She said hi to Leroy and Amelia and scratched them both under their chins for just a second.

She went to sit down on the couch next to Blankets Mountain. Gramma reminded her to always look before she sits on the couch just in case I didn't make to my usual spot to do business. She looked and it was safe, so she sat down and kept on giving me luvins while she talked to gramma. I decided I liked her and I would call her Grammy so I wouldn't get them mixed up when I talked about them to my Facebook friends. Gramma told her about the house and then showed her around. She helped her get her things into the guest bedroom and told her mum would be home in a couple of hours. Grammy said she was tired from the long drive, so she would just sit down at dad's desk and play some games while she waited for mum and dad to get home.

Grace decided she would take advantage of Grammy not knowing how smart and persistent that

137

she could be. She sat next to grammy and when she finished with a treat she kept poking her in the leg with her nose. Then she'd whine and hop up and try to nuzzle Grammy's arm. She even used her nose like when she did the pit maneuver in order to pick her hand up off the computer mouse. Grammy would stop and ask her what she wanted. It didn't take long for her to realize Grace wanted more treats. She gave in, of course, and gave everyone another round of treats. Once she was done, she sat back down and figured Grace would behave. She was wrong. Grace kept it up nonstop until mum got home.

Once mum got home and they said hellos, Grammy told mum about how Grace had been nonstop begging for treats. Mum fussed at Grace and told Grammy that Grace was a very smart dog and could usually figure out how to get people to do what she wanted; especially when it came to getting extra treats and bones. She told Grammy that she would just have to tell Grace no and be firm so she would eventually go lie down and behave.

Grammy went into her room for a minute and when she came back she brought out a whole bunch of hand crocheted cat mats. They were really pretty and made of different yarn. Some of them were super soft and she let me sniff all of them. Grammy said I could have as many as I wanted and that she wanted to donate the rest of them to a local cat shelter. Mum and Grammy went through them and I got to pick out my most favorite ones. Mum told Grammy that she had to work the next day, but on Sunday they could take them to Floyd Felines and Friends which was a local shelter that she occasionally volunteered at.

Grammy thought that was a great idea and she got out her crochet hook to start working on a blanket she hadn't finished yet.

Dad got home at about the same time mum started feeding me my dinner. Dad gave Grammy a big hug and they sat down in the living room to catch up on things. Mum told dad to look at all the cat mats that Grammy brought and he thought they were excellent and that I would absolutely love them. Boy was he right! I thought she must have a heart of gold to make all those mats for kitties that need homes.

Grammy was amazed at how mum was feeding me. She never saw a cat sit quite like I did and be so patient about anything before. She was fascinated by how mum would pile the food up like a mountain and I'd chomp the top off over and over again. Well I didn't feel like I was being patient I was just happy mum was giving me my dinner. When I was full I stood up and turned around to let them know I was ready to go back to Blankets Mountain. Grammy thought that was funny and she just couldn't get over how well I was able to communicate what I wanted.

Once my dinner was finished, mum air-lifted me to the couch where I did my business. Grammy got another surprise at that point. She she said I was one very potent little boy. She then pinched off her nose while mum finished cleaning up. Grammy was amazed that something as small as me could create something that smelled so bad, it could cause a room to be evacuated. Ha, I was proud of myself for being able to impress her so much. She just got here and she was in for a whole weekend of being impressed.

Once the smelled aired out we got to start couch time even earlier than normal. It didn't take me long to impress her again but in a different way. Dad decided to show her my superhero skills with feathers time and she was really amazed. She just couldn't believe how high on the cushions I could jump and how much fun I was having. She laughed and thought it was wonderful how much I obviously loved life and how eager I was to engage with anyone and anything. She couldn't believe my disability didn't cause me to slow down.

I never did let my neurological disease get in the way of having fun and enjoying life. I knew I couldn't do things like Leroy and Amelia racing around the house but I had my entire Blankets Mountain to climb on, and hundreds of feathers to play with. Sometimes I had to do things a little slower or think of a way to overcome my limitations, but I still did what I wanted when I wanted to. Grammy said she just couldn't get over how much life I had in me and she said she could just see the happiness and love shine out of my eyes.

Grammy was the first one up the next morning. She made her morning coffee, came over to check the couch for any surprises, and sat down next to me to give me some luvins. She talked to me for a bit. I gave her the eyes long enough that she walked over to mums drawer to get the bag of treats. Leroy and Amelia heard the bag crackle and they ran to the living room at full speed to get some too.

Mum and dad got up just a little while later. Dad took Grace out and mum made her cup of coffee. Dad came back in, fed Grace and filled up Leroy and

Amelia's bowls while he waited on his own coffee. They sat in the living room and talked for a while and when mum finished her coffee, she got my food ready to feed me breakfast. Grammy still thought it was just amazing how they'd figured out the perfect way to feed me.

They made breakfast and when they were done mum said she had to go to work. She wouldn't be home until early evening. That meant dad would be feeding me dinner and I'd get to impress Grammy again with my potent surprises. Dad and Grammy sat and talked until lunch time. Then, they left to go do "people things" that they'd been talking about the night before.

While they were gone Leroy decided he wanted to go check out Grammy's things in the guest room. Grammy had said that she had a cat allergy. She said she would be fine for the time she was visiting but she'd have to keep the rest of the cats out of the bedroom. As long as she didn't sleep on a blanket the cats had been on she thought she would fine.

Leroy wasn't used to the bedroom door being closed and he didn't like it. He clawed at the bottom of the door and hooked his paws under it and shook it as hard as he could. I watched him from the top of Blankets Mountain and I told him he should quit but he had it in his head that he was going to get the door open. He worked at it for a really long time and he did manage to get it to open up. He went in and I'm sure he did his snooping. He didn't stay in there long before he came back out. For all the effort he put in I thought he was pretty silly about not being in there longer. He just didn't like a closed door.

When dad and Grammy got home, they noticed the open door right away. Grammy went in to look but neither Leroy nor Amelia was in there. Dad told her about Leroy not liking a closed door and showed her how to better latch the door because it didn't always shut right. He got the vacuum out and ran it through the bedroom real quick. Grammy said that should be enough to keep her allergies from bothering her too much.

Grammy went to the kitchen and started cooking. It didn't take long for the whole house to start smelling really good. Dad hoisted me to my ledge and helped me eat dinner while grammy finished up in the kitchen. Mum got home shortly afterwards and she asked what was cooking because it smelled delicious. Grammy told her dad asked for her homemade chicken and dumplings so they'd gone to the grocery store while they were out to get what she needed. I sure was hoping for a bite of that chicken because mum was right! It really did smell delicious.

Mum made sure I got some of the chicken and it was very delicious. Mum gave me a bit and I took it gently from her. Then I gave it a savage shake to make sure it was tenderized. Then I chomped it like it was one of my feathers. I got a few pieces of the chicken and Grammy even made sure Grace, Leroy and Amelia got some too.

We got to have early couch time again that night. Grammy worked on her crocheting while they all chatted. They'd had a good time that day. Dad took granny to a museum in town that he had been to a few years ago when he took his nephew there for a school field trip. Grammy thought it was neat that a small

142

community like we lived had something like that so close. She said she was really impressed by all of the dinosaur fossils and the giant telescopes they had. While they talked about their plans for the next day, Grammy kept giggling while she watched me play with my feathers.

The next day, mum and Grammy got up early and went to the cat shelter to donate Grammy's cat mats. Dad slept in a little later and gave me my breakfast. He worked at his Fantasy Football stuff at his computer like he always did before the games got started. Mum and Grammy got home just as the games started and they ate some more of those chicken dumplings for lunch. Of course, Grammy made sure I got a couple of pieces of that yummy chicken and she laughed when I gently took it right out of her fingers, only to give it a savage shake. Grammy had a good time at the shelter and she said she would start working on making even more cat mats to donate to them. The rescuers were super grateful for the donations and told her they could never have enough of those soft, silky cat mats.

They stayed home the rest of the day and watched some football and talked. We got to have couch time almost all day long that day and I was thinking that grammy should stay more often because I was getting a ton of feathers time and extra treats. I think Grace felt the same way because I'd never seen her get that many treats before. Leroy tried getting into grammy's room a couple more times that day but as soon as dad heard him rattle the door he told Grace to go get him and he wound up getting the pit maneuver and run off. Grammy laughed hard at seeing the pit maneuver.

The next day was pretty much the same with lots of extra treats and luvins. Dad took mum and Grammy out to lunch and when they got back, I found out they had seafood. Grammy sure did like it and she said they had to go back the next time she came. They all ordered crab legs and Grammy even saved me a little bite. I loved it and started planning how I could convince her next time to bring me back my very own crab leg.

They watched movies for the rest of the day and I heard Grammy talking about leaving in the morning. I wished that she could stay because I had so much fun, but mum and dad were both going back to work and she had only planned a short trip. I had quite a wonderful weekend. I learned I had two grammas and got to eat some seriously yummy chicken. I got extra luvins and belly rubs and more couch time than ever before. I was so happy when she said she would be coming back and I always looked forward to her visits.

Neuro Dan - Feather Dan

November 22, 2015 ·

Whoa! Mum got out this big green thing that looks like a tree but it has colored lights and flashy stuffs on it! Leroy gotz in trouble cuz he tried to climb it so he iz pouting in another room. I can't stop staring at it. Humans are so funny sometimes. I luvs you and please sleep with the angels my furiends.

I always enjoyed keeping mum on her toes. She always got so worked up and nervous if she thought I was getting too adventurous. One night, I made her nervous and laugh at the same time. I got a notion and decided to go on another adventure. I climbed up onto the edge of the couch that's closest to mums desk. Then I made my way onto the end table with the lamp. The table doesn't have much traction for me to keep my balance on, so I did slip a little, but I made it across and climbed onto the arm of her desk chair.

From there, I climbed all the way down to the cushion. Then I scaled up the back of the chair until I got to the very top. I walked over to the lamp, stretched out, sniffed the lamp shade and gave it a big goose honk. Mum didn't know what to think about this, but it got her laughing really hard. I then backed down the chair and made my way back across the slippery end table to lie back down on the couch. I looked at mum, gave her a smile then rolled upside down for her to come give me belly rubs. I figured that would help to keep her on her toes.

Later that day, mum went out onto the porch and rummaged inside the storage closet for a while. When she came back in she was dragging this big green thing that had parts falling off. The parts that were falling off while she dragged it across the floor looked like pine tree limbs. She set it down and finished taking it out the box. As strange is it sounded and as hard as it was to believe I was sure it looked like a tree.

She moved some things around in the dining room and pushed the table over to the wall. After she made space she started putting the tree together, which I thought looked like quite the process. It was almost as tall as the ceiling. Once she got it all put together, it did indeed look like a very nice tree, but I couldn't figure out why in the world she was putting a tree in the house.

I wondered what dad was going to say when he got home from work. I mean, he left for work this morning and when he comes home there's a tree in the middle of the house? I'd be pretty surprised if I were him too. Grace was having a good time sniffing it and watching mum. Leroy and Amelia were fascinated as well. Amelia was watching from the table where her food bowl was and Leroy was getting right up in the middle of the whole operation.

Mum then went back out to the porch storage closet and came back in with another big box. She set it on the floor and started taking all sorts of other boxes out and setting them on the table. She got this long bundle of cords and started wrapping them around the tree. I just could not understand what she thought she was doing. This was definitely an odd day. It took her a little while to get the cord completely wrapped around the tree and when she plugged it in to the wall, the entire tree lit up with different colored lights that were blinking.

I was so surprised that I stood up and shook my head. I couldn't believe my eyes! Mum made the tree shine with pretty lights. She must have some secret magic powers she's been hiding. She started taking things out of the smaller boxes that were on the table and hanging them on the tree. I was getting more and more interested because those looked like they might be fun to check out. Leroy must have thought the same thing because he did try to grab one, but mum fussed at him. He got a little miffed but didn't go very

147

far. I was pretty sure he was going to try again as soon as mum turned her back.

Once she was done, she packed up all the empty boxes back into the big box and took it back out to the porch closet. When she came back in, she looked at me and asked me what I thought. I didn't know what to think, I mean she just put a tree in the middle of the house and made it have blinking lights. I thought it was pretty interesting; that was for sure, but I still didn't know why. She picked me up and carried me over to it so I could sniff it and check out the things that she hung on it. There weren't any feathers on it so I decided that I would leave it alone and just be happy to look admire it from afar.

Leroy didn't have the same intentions as me, and when mum turned around to set me down he got under it and started climbing up inside it. Mum heard the racket he was making and turned around to scold him good. She gave him a good enough talking-to that he ran off to the guest bedroom with hurt feelings.

When dad came home I waited anxiously to see his reaction. He walked in, looked at it and told mum that she did a great job. He said he thought it looked really nice! I was dumfounded. How could he not have been absolutely shocked that there was a tree right in the middle of the dining room? He asked mum if I liked the Christmas tree and if Leroy or Amelia had tried to get into it yet. Mum told him about Leroy's scolding and said that so far Amelia was content to look at it. He said he would find a way to tie it to the wall so it wouldn't get knocked over again this year.

So I took all of this to mean they have actually put a tree in the middle of the house before. People sure do some very odd things. It was pretty to look at though, so I thought it would be fun. Plus, I'd get to watch Leroy explore it at night and I wondered just how much trouble he would end up getting himself into. I could also tell that Amelia had her eye on things but I was guessing she was smart enough to wait until mum and dad were in bed.

It was a good thing dad figured out how to secure the tree to the wall because sure enough, once they went to bed, Amelia was quick to join Leroy in some Christmas tree shenanigans. He went right back to doing what he got in trouble for, which was trying to climb right up the middle of it. Amelia decided to see what the low hanging ornaments would sound like if they got pulled down and batted around.

Leroy wound up getting himself stuck in a bunch of the lighting cord about a third of the way up. I was surprised the noise he was making did not wake Grace up yet. By the time he managed to get himself unstuck and out of the tree, the lights on the front were a tangled mess and there were a dozen ornaments on the ground. Once he was back on the ground, he shook his head and strutted off to the guest bedroom like nothing had happened.

Amelia happily enjoyed the ornaments that Leroy knocked down. She played with each of them for a minute or two. She discovered the little wire hooks could come off and she would swat at them until she could get them separated. She wound up with decorations scattered all over the kitchen floor and down the hallway towards the front door.

Dad happened to get up first in the morning and was the first to discover the calamity. He walked past me with a groan and was mumbling something that was probably one of those things mum would make me cover my ears over. He got the coffee started and started picking up the mess. Leroy and Amelia made it a point to stay far out of site. Dad looked over at me and asked me if they really had to pull the hooks off the ornaments. I had to agree with dad; knocking so many down seemed like it should have been enough to quiet that kitty voice that encourages us and makes us do such things but Amelia just lost it when she figured out those hooks came off.

Dad was in the process of putting his second armful of ornaments back on the tree when mum came out of the bedroom. She knew right away what happened and when she looked down the hall towards the front door, she said loudly a word I should have covered my ear for. It took both of them a minute to put the decorations back up and mum didn't like the way the tree looked. She said she'd arrange it better when she got home from work. Dad told her that they probably wouldn't have a choice because they both knew this was just round one.

Dad said Amelia and Leroy were hiding, so mum said it was time for a family meeting. She went to the kitchen closet, got a cup full of cat food, and filled up the cat bowls. Everyone knows no cat can resist the sound of food hitting a bowl first thing in the morning. And sure enough, they both came running out of the second bedroom.

When they jumped up on the table to get to the food bowl mum started asking them what they had done. Amelia completely ignored her but Leroy had a guilty look on his face. Mum pointed to the tree and said that what they did was bad. Amelia just cared about her food, but poor Leroy and his sensitive feelings sulked off into the second bedroom. I felt bad for the big guy because we cats really just can't resist that voice that tells us to do those types of things. I reminded him that mum didn't even raise her voice, so he should toughen up a little. Dad noticed the retreat to the bedroom and told her Leroy would be sulking again. Mum said he'd be back for luvins when she got home because with Thanksgiving only two days away, he'd be sure to be okay once she started cooking tomorrow. They both hoped the tree would survive for a while. Grace was whining and poking dad in the leg repeatedly and he realized that with being distracted by the tree fiasco, he'd forgotten to take her out.

They disappeared out the door and mum stopped to say good morning. I wanted to know what Thanksgiving was because the name alone sounded truly wonderful. I felt like it summed up my entire year. I knew I was very young but I'd never had more to give thanks for in my entire life. She must have known what I was thinking because she sat down with me and told me all about it.

Of all the holidays I'd learned about so far, I thought that Thanksgiving was the best one by far. That people would take a day out of the year to break their routines, meet together and take time to be thankful for each other and what they have was inspiring. Sometimes people managed to impress me, and that so many people, no matter who they were or where they came from, understood the value of giving thanks made me believe that the entire world was a better place than I thought before I learned of the holiday. People sure could be full of surprises.

Leroy sulked that day but after mum and dad went to bed, he came out of the other bedroom and was right back at the tree. He was a little more careful and did manage to avoid knocking half of the ornaments off. He told me he really wasn't sulking; he just wanted to make mum feel guilty because he knew he'd get some extra people food soon if he held out until then. He was being sneaky and I reminded him about what Thanksgiving was supposed to be about. He gave me a tail twitch and walked off.

When mum started cooking the next day the entire house started to smell amazing. She was talking to dad about what everyone was planned to bring for the feast. Mum and dad were going to be making mums family recipe of baked beans, dad's family recipe of a dessert called apple pancake soufflé, mashed potatoes and squash casserole. Mums sister was hosting and making baked ham, green beans, a dessert called "dirt cake" and getting all of the relish trays together. Gramma and Gramma-great were making cornbread, the turkey and turkey stuffing.

It sure sounded like a feast to me. Leroy said everyone would have leftovers for a week and we'd be able to get some of the turkey and maybe even some ham. Mum kept on talking about even more different food that they'd have and that she was looking forward to. Between the smells from mum cooking and listening to all of the different foods I was hoping I'd get to try all of it.

I wondered what happened to all of those turkey feathers. If millions of people were going to be having turkey on one day, then surely there must be enough feathers around that every cat everywhere should get to have feathers time Thanksgiving. I planned on having a talk with mum about that because it would just be a waste for all of those good chomping feathers to be thrown out.

Early on Thanksgiving, mum and dad gathered up all of the food they'd been cooking and got it ready to go. It took them both two trips to get it all to the car. As much as I wasn't a fan of car rides, I tried to get mum to take me when she came to give me goodbye luvins. She promised she would come back with plenty of yummy surprises for me.

She wasn't exaggerating either. When they got back, it took them both two trips again to get everything back in the house. Mum had all the food spread out across the kitchen counter and told dad it was going to be a challenge to get it all to fit in the refrigerator. Grace must have been able to smell the food through the containers because she was tail wagging and jumping up and down, trying to see the loot on the kitchen counter.

Dad put Grace's leash on her and just about had to drag her outside to do her business. Amelia was on the kitchen table paying very close attention and Leroy decided that it was time to come out and start being nice to mum again. He was rubbing up against her legs so she would make sure not to miss him. She

153

reached down and scratched him on his head and told him to be patient.

Dad came back in and between the two of them, they managed to get everything in the refrigerator. Mum came over to the couch and called Leroy and Amelia. Grace was right on mum's heel poking her in the leg. Dad called Grace into the kitchen and she ran fast like she was in pursuit to get to him. I was pretty sure Grace was getting some people food because dad was making her work for it; telling her to sit and lay down. After a couple of commands, I could hear her jaws snapping and chomping.

Once Leroy and Amelia were around mum, she started handing each of us a tiny little piece of turkey. I never had turkey like that before and I loved it! We all got a piece of turkey and wanted more. Then, mum said no more but she got us some special turkey flavored turkey treats that she would give us after I got my dinner. I didn't see what was wrong with having the turkey for dinner, but that was okay. She said there would be more treats after dinner so I had something to look forward to.

Grace ran back into the kitchen with a big ole' bone dad said was a ham bone. He turned on the T.V. and turned the channel to a football game. I got excited because it wasn't even Sunday and there was football on T.V. I hoped that meant I'd get extra play time and treats like I did every football Sunday. Dad fixed up the couch and sat down next to me. He waited for mum to go back into the kitchen, and then he snuck me a tiny little piece of turkey.

Mum came back into the living room and sat down with me and dad. She watched the game with us and we all spent the rest of the day lounging on the couch, spending time together. I sure knew what I was thankful for. I didn't need a special day for me to remember though. It was something that I thought about every single day.

Mum told me that most people thought about it more than once a year too, but not like I did. I guess it was because of how my life had been less than a year ago and how happy I was now. Even though I knew I had a disease that meant I might not have a long life, I just couldn't imagine asking for anything different. Dad always said he could just look into my eyes and see my love of life radiating out and into the world. It made me feel good to know that mum and dad could look into my eyes and see how happy I was. After all, if they hadn't taken a chance on me my life might have already been over already.

Chapter Nineteen – Holidays

Neuro Dan - Feather Dan
December 25, 2015 ·
*Merry Christmas everyone! I really like
Christmas. So many new toys and FEATHERS and
I've never seen so many Temptations ever! I also
found out that my brother Leroy likes the wrapping
paper and he likes to hide in the gift bags. He's silly!
Mum says I can have a new FEATHER every day now
if I want. My friends you are all amazing and I love*

you. I hope you all had a wonderful day filled with loved ones. Sleep with the angels tonight.

I thought Leroy had exaggerated but he was absolutely right. We all enjoyed Thanksgiving leftovers for an entire week. Dad finally figured out that I was better off with just the turkey treats mum had gotten and not the actual turkey because after just a couple of days of him sneaking bits of it to me when he gave Grace some, I started getting really gassy.

It never failed; I would get the worst of my gas at night, always just in time for everyone to sit down on the couch. Dad would wave his hands and groan. Sometimes he would even get up and move to the other side of the living room. He tried burning incense and lighting candles but mum just laughed at him. She said I was a potent little boy and he was going to have to live with it. It didn't bother mum as much because she sat on a different part of the couch but I got dad every time.

A couple of times dad got to laugh at mum. I'd given her the eyes so good that she gave me a bit more turkey. She didn't know that dad had been sneaking me little pieces. That night dad got up to get away from the smell. My tummy had been making weird noises so I snuck behind mum and took care of some extra business. Mum heard it and smelled it at the same time, so she jumped up off the couch like she'd been stung by a bee.

It was quite a mess and I wound up with a sink bath. Mum grabbed me and told dad to get the towels. I knew it was pretty bad and mum moved so fast I barely had a chance to protest. Dad got the blankets

157

on the couch in the laundry and everything cleaned up right about the time mum was finishing with me.

It was a good thing that the leftovers were almost done because mum decided right then that I was done getting any more people food for a while. Dad agreed and was waving a smoking incense stick around the living room trying to fix the smell. Mum said I needed to get back to my normal diet and nothing extra until Christmas.

Over the next week mum and dad kept mentioning Christmas. Mum must have thought I knew what she was talking about because unlike Thanksgiving, she didn't sit down and explain to me. I was trying to figure it all out on my own but all I could tell was they were trying to decide what to get different people.

Leroy said it was a fun holiday because mum and dad always got us kitty's new toys to play with and treats. He also told me that the family all got together again like they did on Thanksgiving and had another feast. He mentioned that it did seem to mean more to people than it did to cats. He mentioned that part of the day was kind of serious and part of the day was lots of fun. He didn't understand it either but told me mum would make sure we'd have a great day.

I started getting quite a bit of mail that week. Unlike most times when I got mail, mum would take the packages and put them under the Christmas tree. She said I was going to have to wait until Christmas morning to open them up. She made sure to let my Facebook friends know that the gifts they were sending had arrived and that they were stowed safely under the tree.

Grace got extra curious about a couple of the packages and one night she tried to get into one. She was having a difficult time being quiet about it and Leroy heard the noise. He came to check it out, and soon Amelia was there too. I watched from Blankets Mountain as she managed to get the box pulled apart. Once she got inside the box, there was a pouch with some treats in it. I'm not sure how she could have smelled the treats through the box and wrappings but she managed to gnaw at it like she did on her bones until it opened. Then, she ate all of the treats! Leroy and Amelia tried to get a few of them too but Grace growled and wouldn't let them have any.

That was the first time I ever saw Grace get into something like that. She sure was determined though and kept at it all night until she got to the prizes inside. If she would have asked, I would have been happy to share treats with her. I figured I wouldn't give her a hard time about getting one of my presents this time because I knew I'd have plenty later on. When mum got up in the morning and saw the mess, Grace got in trouble.

Mum must have been a great detective because she knew immediately that it had been Grace. After mum fussed at her, Grace lowered her head and snuck off to the bedroom. Mum decided that the presents would have to stay in a box on the top shelf in a closet until Christmas morning. I supposed that was a good idea but it was fun to look at everything under the tree.

Mum had been working extra hard that week. Her school work seemed like it had been taking a lot more time than usual and she was busy with work on top of that. She said she was working on a very difficult and important paper. I was sure to tell her that feathers are much more fun to spend time with. Dad spent extra time trying to help with getting me fed and taking care of the house work so she wouldn't have to worry about it. People sure seem to find some strange things to spend so much time on.

She even took an entire day off to try to get the paper done. She looked really stressed out but she told me that it was due that night. She also said she would get a winter break when she finished it and then she would be able to spend a lot more time giving me luvins. She took several breaks that day and came to spend time with me. I made sure to purr and give her lots of wet faced mushes so I could see her smile. She finally got it done and she and dad went out to dinner to celebrate.

When they got home, mum had a big hand full of packages that had come in the mail. Mum sat down and read my Christmas cards to me. I loved the messages my friends would write. They were so sweet and some of them even made mums eyes water. She got to one card and asked dad to go get a specific package. She said that the friend who sent that card also sent a package and they asked her to let me open it before Christmas.

It took dad a minute to find it but he came in the living room and set it down next to me. Mum opened it up for me and I sniffed at the wrappers. Once she opened the box, I peeked inside. There was a blue squeaky shoe toy, a yellow feather toy and a bag of real feathers for me to chomp on. I stayed busy playing with those toys all night that night and I had a great time.

I kept getting more and more packages in the mail. Mum told me that either she or dad had to be sure to check the mail every single day. She said I was getting so much stuff that the mail man was obviously having a hard time figuring out where to put everything. The dozen or so parcel boxes that were at the mail boxes were getting filled up pretty quick.

That Sunday, mum decided that she was going to spend all day grooming me. My disability made it hard for me to get all of my fur perfect. Mum was really good about helping me out by combing me every couple of days. She had been so busy with that term-paper that she had gotten a little behind. She wound up with a pile of fur that she said was about as big as me. I felt much better afterwards, but I always gave her a couple of love bites to remind her to take a break. She always laughed at this, told me she was sorry, and gave me the break I wanted.

When mum took breaks from my grooming, dad would be sure to play with me and give me some treats. He even interrupted mum a couple of times because his teams scored and that meant I got treats. He and mum were trying to decide who had enough time to get the mail the next day. Dad said the mail man surely was exhausted. Not only did he have to deliver people mail which was extremely busy for him already but this year he was getting my mail too. Dad said I got more packages than twenty people would so he hoped that the mail man got lots of rest on his day off today.

I felt so much better after mum got done grooming me that the next morning, I wound up getting a notion. I waited for mum and dad to go to work and I decided that I would go on a floor adventure. I explored a lot that day. I even checked out the Christmas tree and packages that were under it. Leroy said that Christmas was just a couple of days away and that they would take the tree down a few days afterwards. I figured I could at least go give it a sniff and try to figure out why Leroy thought it was so much fun.

It was interesting but not feathers interesting so I decided to keep on exploring. Grace kept an eye on me but I never had to worry about her doing that infamous pit maneuver because I couldn't go fast enough to get her worked up. It took most of the day to explore because I had to stop and take lots of breaks but I even got all the way into the bedroom. The bedroom was big and I didn't feel like exploring that much. Plus, I knew Leroy liked the bedroom so I figured it was kind of like his Blankets Mountain. I decided it would only be polite to respect his space.

Instead of the bedroom, I decided to explore the big closet at the end of the hall. Mum had lots of boots and shoes in there and dad had some boxes. I didn't know what was in the boxes but they didn't smell like feathers so they didn't interest me. I managed to get all the way back in the closet where mum had some boots lined up when I got the idea that I should play hide and seek again.

No sooner had the thought crossed my mind when I heard a key in the front door and it opened up. Grace barked and darted to the door but it was mum so she started wagging her tail. Mum grabbed her leash and took her outside real quick. While she was doing that, I took a second to get hidden real good behind her tall boots. Mum went to find me and give me luvins and when I wasn't there she started calling me.

I could hear her saying my name and checking all of my normal spots. She checked under her desk, behind the blinds by the glass door, under dad's desk, and under the kitchen table. She even started checking places she knew I wouldn't go like the kitchen and the second bedroom. She looked in her bedroom, under the bed and even checked in the closet that I was in but I was hidden so good she didn't see me.

She got so upset that she called dad and told him she'd looked everywhere and couldn't find me. Dad checked the security camera on his phone and told her that I had to be somewhere that no one had been there. She kept looking, but she looked for an hour and still couldn't find me. I was starting to think I was going to have to just come out because she was getting upset but then I heard dad come home and I just couldn't resist seeing how he would search for me.

Dad checked all of the places that mum checked. Mum took apart Blankets Mountain to make sure I wasn't playing that trick again. Dad got an idea and he called Grace. He asked Grace where I was and asked her to look for me. Grace barked and looked all over Blankets Mountain. Dad kept telling her to find me and she ran around sniffing everywhere. She finally got to the closet sniffed around, found me then came back out and started wagging her tail.

Dad came in and checked the closet. He did more than look though. He got down on his hands and knees and started moving everything around. When he moved mums boots there I was sitting pretty with a great big smile. He left me where I was and called for mum. When mum saw me she called me a stinker, told me not to ever scare her like that again and scooped me up. I got a whole lot of luvins before dinner time.

There was some very bad weather that night. I was watching the news with dad and it was so bad and covered such a big area that I got worried about my friends. Mum and dad were talking about how horrible it was for people to lose everything just two days before Christmas. Mum called them tornadoes and she assured me that we would send good thoughts and prayers to my Facebook friends that night. I made sure to stay snuggled close with mum. The house felt like it was shaking because of all of the thunder boomers, and I didn't like that at all. It turned out that all of our friends were safe but we all sent prayers to those who weren't so lucky.

The day before Christmas reminded me very much of the day before Thanksgiving. Mum cooked lots of food again and I really liked how good it made the house smell. When dad got home from work, he helped mum in the kitchen and took care of getting me my dinner. Mum told me about this guy named Santa Claus that I'd been hearing so much about. She said that Santa spent that night delivering presents to children all over the world. She said he had a giant magical sleigh that was pulled by a bunch of reindeer and that the one in the front was special like me. She said he had a special nose that glowed so bright that it helped Santa see in the dark!

I was pretty amazed. I wondered if I sat on my steps by the glass door that night if I could see him. There were houses behind us that were down a hill and I could see the roofs of those houses, so I'd have a terrific vantage point. Then mum told me he would only deliver toys once all of the children were in bed. She told me I needed to be sure to go to sleep early that night so I wouldn't scare off Santa. She didn't want all of the children in the neighborhood to miss out on their presents because I was up and looking.

I thought that it would be pretty sad if I spoiled Christmas for the children so I decided I would just go to bed. Mum told me that for being a good boy, I could open up one of my presents before I went to bed and then the rest of them Christmas morning. Mum opened my present for me and it had a package of treats. So that night, we all got to enjoy a few more tasty treats.

Christmas morning was one amazing experience. Mum and dad made several trips to the closet where mum had hidden the presents. By the time they had them all out on the couch with me. The stack was as tall as Blankets Mountain! I got so many new toys and feathers that I could never describe them all in one day. Leroy and Amelia got some packages addressed to them too. When everything was opened I sat up. Mum then piled them in a giant circle around me. Dad said I looked like a proud dragon sitting on a mountain of gold. There were so many toys; I didn't even know what to play with first.

Mum left me in the middle of my pile that dad said was the biggest pile of Christmas loot he'd ever seen. They started getting all of the food they'd been cooking together and went over to mum's sister's house. They were gone for quite a while and when they came home, I could smell all of the yummy leftovers that they had. I hoped that dad had forgotten about the gassy experience from Thanksgiving and that I would get lots of leftovers again.

As it would turn out, I didn't get leftovers. They didn't have turkey that time. Leroy said that turkey seemed to be just for Thanksgiving and that some people even called it turkey day. They had ham instead and mum said I wasn't supposed to eat ham. I didn't mind. I got so many new treats that morning when I opened my presents that I knew I'd be getting something yummy all the time. Grace got another ham bone and anytime Leroy or Amelia tried to sniff it she would snarl and growl at them.

Mum said that the next week was going to be full of fun. Dad's birthday was in just a few days. Leroy said dad wasn't as sensitive about his age as mum and most ladies were. Mum picked at him a bit, telling him he was turning into an old man. On top of dad's birthday, she said later that week it was going to be New Year's Eve and 2015 would be another year in the history books.

I was excited for dad's birthday but was a bit confused about the New Year thing. Leroy let me know that people were obsessed with time. He said that they even wore watches on their arms to keep track of it. He said that while the only part of time we cats really cared about was things like dinner time, feathers time, and snuggles time but humans tracked and recorded everything. He said that every year on the same date they decided it would be useful to start another year all over again.

He didn't get it and neither did I but I did enjoy joining mum, dad and all of my Facebook friends with celebrating all of these holidays and traditions. I thought that it was good for people to have times set aside to remember things and spend time together. I thought about how busy mum and dad always seemed to be and realized the rest of the world was probably just as busy. I wondered if people didn't have those traditions, if they would just forget to stop and remember the parts of life that were what made living worthwhile.

Dad's birthday came pretty quick. Mum said he had a great day because he had won his fantasy football league and won a player-autographed football. He was even trying to decide where he was going to display it and that he was going to have to order a special display case for it. I wasn't sure what that meant but it sure did make him happy which made me and mum happy too.

Another tradition that the family had was that on a person's birthday the entire family went out to eat somewhere and they celebrated by spending time together. A whole bunch of the family got together and they went out to dinner to celebrate dad's birthday. When mum and dad came home mum had saved a little bit of steak and let me try it. I really liked that and wished we could have that more often. I was starting to get the idea that food was a very important part of all of the human traditions. I thought it was odd but I was happy that it was because they always made really good food on those special days.

That night, during couch time, mum told me that there was something that people did that I wouldn't like on New Year's Eve. She told me that, just like during the fourth of July, there would be fireworks. She said it would be different this time because everyone would wait until midnight to set them off. Mum and dad knew how badly the noise from fireworks scared me. They talked about what they would do with me for the night. Dad said they would have to think about it and come up with something.

As it turned out, on New Year's Eve, I got to spend the night in the bedroom with mum and dad. They both had to get up early for work the next day and had decided they wouldn't stay up for the festivities that year. Dad was a little bit nervous about me sleeping in the bed with them. He was worried one of them would roll over on me and he knew I wouldn't be able to get away like a normal cat. Mum told him I would be fine. Then he said he was worried I'd do my business on the bed and mum told him not to worry, that I wouldn't and if I did they'd just get it cleaned up. Dad agreed that he'd rather not have me alone and scared. They decided that if either of them woke up after the noise died down they could take me back to Blankets Mountain.

For the first time ever I was able to lie in bed snuggled in between mum and dad. They both fell asleep pretty quickly but I wasn't tired. I had gotten lots of sleep during the day and really only took little naps at night. That was okay because I had never felt like I was in a safer place. When the fireworks started I knew that meant that it was the New Year so I guess it was officially 2016. That sure sounded strange to me but so did a lot of things that people do.

The house right behind us set off a lot of really loud fireworks and it went on for almost an hour. Grace barked a little and wiggled her way under the bed to try to get away from the noise. I'm not sure where Leroy or Amelia went but I knew they were used to it. Mum rolled over when it was getting really loud and stroked my head and ears. She whispered sweet words to me and then she fell back asleep.

The noise eventually stopped and the night got quiet. I did a lot thinking that night. I had come so far that year. I still missed JuJu and wondered how she was. I hoped that KT was doing well. I prayed that all of the other cats at Misfits were okay and she was finding them homes. I even wanted the couple of bully cats there to find the same kind of loving home I had. I believed that if they could experience the love of a family in a forever home that they wouldn't feel like they had to be bullies anymore.

I thought back on my trip to my new home, meeting Grace for the first time and that indignant butt sniff she gave me. I never thought I'd have my very own dog for a bodyguard but I did and couldn't have asked for better.

I thought back on all of those trips to the vet. There sure were a lot of those and I was glad they were behind me. For just a minute I thought about my disease and that the doctors said I would be lucky to live two years. I was so happy that I just couldn't imagine not being here with mum and dad, Grace, Leroy and Amelia. I had so many friends on Facebook and I so enjoyed telling them my stories. I

169

wanted to be able to tell my stories for many years. I had my very own Blankets Mountain and mum said I now had so many feathers that I could have a new one every night for a very long time.

Plus, I still had so much that I had to get figured out. I didn't think I knew what all of those holidays and traditions were yet and I just had to know about all of them. It was so exciting to get my packages in the mail. I knew there would be other kitties out there that were scared, hurt and needed help. I wanted to be able to use my Facebook page to help them. There was still one thing that I was the most curious about and I just had to get it figured out. I had to know why Leroy and Amelia did those odd patrols every single night, all night long. I had to know the answer to that.

I had so much I wanted to live for. I loved my life so much but if it had to be short I would definitely make the most of it. I decided that night that I wanted to be able to spread as much love back to the world as the world had given to me. That would be my mission. Every day I was blessed with life I would help bring light to the dark parts of the world. I would try to be there for anyone who was in a dark place like I had been when I first started my life. I was very determined to show those experts that I would beat the odds.

I didn't sleep much that night but the longer the night went on and the more I thought about things, the better I felt. Snuggled up between mum and dad I had declared my mission to the universe.

I felt like one of those knights in shining armor. Mounted on the back of a mighty steed, standing on top of Blankets Mountain, looking over the land I knew my purpose. Through my stories I would search the world for those dark places. I would charge in on my steed, lance lowered to attack and I would chase away the darkness leaving light, love and hope in its place.

My journey had just begun…

Prologue

Well my friends, thank you so much for listening to my stories. Sharing my stories is my most favorite thing ever. I think I like telling my stories even more than feathers but let's just keep that between us. That was my first year and I thought I would stop here because it seemed fitting with all of the other traditions that we have.

I still have so many more stories that I'd like to tell you. If you'd like to hear them I'll start gathering my thoughts and pick out some of my favorite ones. Oh, and yes, I do figure out why Leroy and Amelia do those odd patrols and you won't believe it!

Made in the USA
Coppell, TX
30 March 2021

52682841R00100